Praise [illegible]
Woman of Worth

"I have known Winonna for more than a decade now, but it seems like a lifetime because we have poured so much life experience together into that time! Our journey has taken us on some powerful life lessons together, and we have both grown as a result. What I cherish most about Winonna is we can both be completely free with each other to speak our truth. There is no pretense or superficiality to it. Winonna has enriched my life in so many ways, even though we can be at odds with each other, as every great friendship experiences from time-to-time. I hope she will always be my sister and friend."

— Mary Borrows, Marysville, Washington

"Winonna was raised in Detroit, married young, and had a marriage that did not last. She has raised children and struggled with alcoholism/addiction, but through virtue of much grit and tenacity, she overcame her addictions and went to college. She has a remarkable capacity for gaining friends of all ages and backgrounds, and she has helped others with their struggles with alcohol, as well as her own daughter who struggles with health issues. She is a remarkable woman, and in her new book, *Woman of Worth*, she shares how she became so incredible."

— Dr. William Purcell, Professor, Seattle Pacific University

"I met Winonna about twelve years ago at an Alcoholics Anonymous meeting. She didn't seem to have anything together, but she had this drive to stay sober. As the years have gone by, I've watched Winonna grow. I've come to the conclusion that if Winonna can stay sober and get her act together, anyone can, including me. In essence, she became my big sister. She went back to school and got a degree. She took care of an adult child and her adult child's children while holding down multiple jobs. She unwittingly became a role model for me. I am happy to have watched her during this journey we call "sobriety," and I look forward to watching her grow more because God knows I need all the help I can get! Thanks, Winonna, for showing me the way."

— Curtis Gregory, Redmond, Washington

"Every now and then, life brings us treasures. This couldn't be more true in regards to the friendship I have cultivated with Winonna Saari. For more than ten years, she has brought a spirit of laughter, resilience, and most of all faith to my life. She lives life authentically with an attitude of adventure, freedom, and a glass half-full. It is a trait that draws many to her, and I am grateful for her friendship."

— Connie Terry, Realtor/Broker at Coldwell Banker Bain, Everett, Washington

"At first, flattery drew me to Winonna. I shouldn't say that, but it's true: she enrolled in the courses I was teaching after hearing me speak at a career event put on by Everett Community College Women's Center. That's flattery for a professor because we want nothing more than to inspire students. She said I did that. I don't remember what I said at that event, but I will always remember Winonna and her incisive smarts, and her willingness to ask questions of anyone in the pursuit of knowledge and the truth. She has a relentlessly active mind that seeks knowledge of all kinds. And she also taught me how to act in movies: get all the goodies and react *out loud*. She's also—via Instagram—shown me how to self-care through travel, family, and forever friendships. I've done some vicarious living through Winonna. I hope we remain friends for life."

— Andrea Otáñez, Educator, Journalist, Writer

"In *Woman of Worth*, Winonna Saari takes us on a rollercoaster ride through her life of addiction and alcoholism, marriage and children, jail and recovery. From drawing on the support of loving family members to making peace with an estranged father, and from finding the strength to go to college and care for an ill adult child to spreading the message that recovery is possible, Winonna has proven that you can turn around your life no matter what road you've gone down and make changes that will make others take notice and want to follow your example. Thank you, Winonna, for being a voice of courage and motivation."

— Tyler R. Tichelaar, PhD and Award-Winning Author of *Narrow Lives* and *The Best Place*

"I have known Winonna for more than ten years. I have watched her transform from a woman controlled by her circumstances and a fragmented childhood to her most genuine powerful self. Her journey has been at times excruciating, and at times gleefully exhilarating. She has accepted the will of some Higher Power bent on carrying her into a totally new life and a new way. She terrifies me and inspires me at the same time by her absolute leap of faith. Terrifies me because she invites me, and everyone who has the courage, to leap with her. Her story of family, love, travels, and addiction is so compelling that I must go along with her, and you will want to also."

— Danny Ventura, Everett, Washington

"*Woman of Worth* is a story of overcoming intergenerational trauma through the power of recovery. There were many moments while reading when I paused to reflect on Winonna's journey through culture, parenting, and relentless self-discovery. This book is a must-read for anyone who has experienced the effects of addiction personally or with their loved ones. I was moved by the author's humility and compassion. It is rare indeed for a book to change your mind and your heart!"

— Amy Socha, Everett, Washington

"I have known Winonna since she was fourteen. I have seen her go through good times and bad times, and even at her lowest, she always climbed right back up and headed to the top. As my BFF, I wish her all the best of luck and success in her new future."

— Marjorie Jackson-Cowans, Detroit, Michigan

"Winonna Saari's story of overcoming addiction, a shattered childhood, and dysfunctional behavior will inspire you to believe anything is possible when you have hope and are willing to change. *Woman of Worth* is a testament to the power that lies within all of us if we only believe in ourselves and accept a little help when it is offered."

— Susan Friedmann, CSP and International Bestselling Author of *Riches in Niches: How to Make It BIG in a small Market*

Woman of Worth

If I Can Recover, Anyone Can

Winonna Saari

New York

Woman of Worth: If I Can Recover, Anyone Can

Published by:

Aviva Publishing
Lake Placid, NY
(518) 523-1320
www.AvivaPubs.com

While this book is based on real events, the names of many people have been changed to protect their privacy.

Address all inquiries to:

Winonna Saari
7401 84th St. N.E
Marysville, WA 98270
(425) 268-5893
saariw@spu.edu
www.WomanofWorthBook.com

ISBN: 978-1-63618-087-8

Library of Congress Control Number: 2021906900

Editors: Tyler Tichelaar and Larry Alexander, Superior Book Productions

Cover Design: Devon Burke

Interior Book Layout: Larry Alexander, Superior Book Productions

Author Photo: Esther Mitchell

Every attempt has been made to source properly all quotes.

"Don't tell me about your addiction,
tell me about your pain."

— Dr. Gabor Maté

Dedication

To all my grandchildren who fill my heart with a joy: Rafael Echauri, Quiren Boyd, Darien Boyd, Jolon Jefferson, Akiera Jefferson, Jazziella Echauri, Azael Echauri, and Alexander Matthew Boyd.

To my sons, who are my heroes, and my daughters, who have beautiful spirits.

To my friend Darlene Barnhart, who always encouraged me to write. Unfortunately, she capitulated to the disease of alcoholism in 2020. Rest in peace, my friend!

Acknowledgments

This book would not have been possible without the support of many people. My deepest gratitude goes to:

Laurie Hardie. Thank you for encouraging me to become an author.

Curtis Gregory. Thank you for your support and wanting me to be successful on my journey.

Devon Burke. Thank you for creating my book cover.

Tracy Mattox. Thank you for your graphic design.

Susan Friedmann, my publisher at Aviva Publishing. Thank you for your belief in my story and your willingness to take me on as a client.

Tyler Tichelaar and Larry Alexander of Superior Book Productions. As my editors, Tyler and Larry took my hodgepodge of stories and experiences and shaped them into a book that is hopefully a gift to help all who read it.

My GoFundMe supporters. Without you, I would not have been able to finance my publishing journey. I appreciate your belief in the importance of my story.

Contents

Introduction

DO YOU THINK YOUR CHILDHOOD SUCKED?

Do you wish your life was different?

Do you experience shame about your past?

Are you doing what you love?

Do you wish you could do whatever you want without anyone complaining?

Do you wish people would stop talking about how messed up you are?

Do you wish you could change?

Do you like what life is showing you?

If you have any of those thoughts and feelings, you've come to the right place. I've had them all and can understand, at least to some degree since we all have different experiences, what you arc going through. In this book, I'll show you how I took those situations and changed my life for the better.

Early in life, I internalized an unspoken message that I was damaged goods and not good enough. I was told I didn't have feelings. I felt unheard, unloved. My emotions developed around fear, rejection, and ridicule. I lived self-exiled. Eventually, I moved far away from home. I carried my exiled self into all my personal relationships. The deep shame, debilitating fear, grief over the have nots and feeling unconnected, and a dependency on drugs and alcohol tumbled me into the abyss of misery. I often felt I had nothing of value to offer anyone. Suicide became an option. I drank and drugged my way through relationships.

For years, I wished and prayed for some sort of relief and normalcy. I would drive to parks and sit on benches to people-watch. I paid close attention to how people responded to each other, especially those who appeared happy and free to be, unlike me. I desired freedom to be, but I had no clue what that looked or felt like. After a series of geographical shuffles, searching for better places to be, and one vivid moment of clarity, a random lady looked at me, started questioning me about my life, and then suggested I find a support group and join it. She went through her rolodex of resources and pointed me toward a group for starters. I decided, out of desperation, to make one last-ditch effort and crawled skeptically into rooms filled with people I did not know. I had never heard of support groups or recovery groups before, but I went. I stayed sober fourteen months with one group—the longest time I had been sober since I was eleven years old. Although I didn't stay sober, I always remembered the experience.

Years later, I found connectedness with a group of people with whom I now have a strong sense of belonging. Their inclusion of me was what I found attractive. The way they talked to me and the way they treated me made a difference. Previous to joining this group, my life had narrowed to isolation, destitution, and a horrible mind-fuck that led to suicidal desperation. I lived my life like an orphan. I didn't feel like I belonged to anyone. During short intervals of being clean and sober, I traveled back and forth from the East Coast to the West Coast, trying to put my life puzzle pieces together—one piece at a time over a long period.

Today, I can see the bigger picture. It's funny how life has its way of forcing turning points. The turning points are mirroring and telling. Researching reasons, examining situations, and questioning my very existence led me to intentionality, the woman I desired to be, the woman I am, a Woman of Worth!

If you have even an inkling of hope within you that you can also improve your life—and I know that inkling exists because it must be why you picked up this book of hope and help—then I hope you will take this journey with me. I hope in my story you will find the courage, strength, and inspiration to find value in your own journey and begin recreating your life for the better. Why do I hope this? Because I believe you are also a woman—or man—of worth.

Please come along with me on this journey. A better life is out there for both of us.

Your friend,

Winonna

CHAPTER 1

Growing Up and Finally Growing Wise

THINGS HAPPENED. AND AS A RESULT, my soul awakened. I don't know if it's a good thing or not that God gave me a good memory to remember the things that happened. My hope is that God can make useful the things that happened to me. I hope I can use my voice and my experience to reach others to let them know what happened to them as children happened to me too. That is why I am writing this book. If you are one of those people, please know you are not alone. I believe I can help you.

My story begins when I was a child and began to have nightmares. In fact, my reality was a nightmare. One nightmare I had was recurring. I have no idea if I had the nightmare because I had watched a scary movie or because I woke up in this one particular place—a place I had been before, but I had not gone there often. This place was unfamiliar in the sense that I only went there at night and I woke up in an unfamiliar bed. I wondered how I ended up in that place. I always seemed to wake up in the middle of the night there. I woke up several times in this bed. I'll never forget it. It was dark. I didn't know for sure where

I was, but I didn't dare to cry out—I knew better. I willed myself to be quiet and go back to sleep. Every time I woke up in this particular room, I had the same routine: I dreamed. The scary clown face dream continually haunted me. In the dream, I willed myself to fight off this scary clown. I kept waking up. I would end up staying awake until daybreak. But one night, the dream was different. The dream changed. It changed from the scary-faced clown I fought off to a recurring dream of seeing flipping pages of a book, like someone was continuously flipping through them.

If a girl like me, who is from the ghetto streets of Detroit, can escape the demons of addiction and shift her life from the hellish depths of alcoholism to being a middle-aged, African American woman who enjoys the fruits of life in recovery, then anyone can. I was once a woman whose face was always scraping the bottom of someone else's shoe, who was frowned upon by society and her family and friends, but I became a woman who reclaimed her dignity through the principles of integrity, hard work, not giving up before the miracle happened, and having a mustard seed of faith. That faith was freely given to me by complete strangers who held out a helping hand. They offered me unconditional love without any expectations or strings attached. They offered me the chance to come along with them, live a life of newfound freedoms and renewed hopes, and I did.

This book tells the story of how I made that incredible change. If you are struggling with the demons of addiction, alcoholism, low self-esteem, or any other issues you can name, this book will give you insight into how to overcome your addictions and gain your power to change.

Honesty Is the Best Policy

When I was about age three, I had a babysitter watching over me. One day, I was walking past my bedroom when I saw the shadow of my sitter. I stood in my bedroom doorway watching her. I witnessed her wrestle with my piggy bank. She was wiggling the folded dollar bills out from the tiny coin hole on the bottom. When she succeeded, she put the money in her bra. Once she turned around and saw me, her eyes changed. Her eyes terrified me. Later, my mom asked me about that money. I told her the babysitter had taken it. I have no idea what the babysitter told her, but every time I was asked about it, I got spanked. That same process went on for days. I repeatedly told my parents the truth about what I had witnessed, and I repeatedly got spanked. I was never believed. I was called a liar every time. I was devastated because honesty was all I knew.

Years later, every time I visited with my family, lots of drinking was involved. I was in my late twenties and partying with one of my sisters. I saw she was intoxicated. I wanted to enhance my party. I went into the pocket of her coat, which was lying beneath where I was sitting, and found cash. I stole the money. I left and bought drugs, then came back and continued partying like I had never left. The party went on for a couple of days. A few days after the partying was over, she called me to ask, "Did you steal my money?" I said, "Yeah, I stole your money." She replied, "You are honest to a fault. I wanted to beat you up, but now I can't because you didn't lie; you are too honest."

I first landed in an Alcoholics Anonymous Twelve-Step program at age twenty-nine. I didn't stick around for long, but what stuck with me was the first principle I learned; it reminded me that honesty was the best policy. I had learned that in preschool. The message I received at home when I was young was honesty came with consequences of punishment, not rewards. I started practicing little lies just to save myself from troubles. During all those years of practicing dishonesty, nothing ever really worked out for me. When I lied, my conscience bothered me. I could not stop thinking about what I did. When I was honest, it, gave me a stronger reason to stand up for what I knew was right, regardless of the outcome. Honesty is still the best policy, no matter what. Struggles are real; be honest about small things.

Not Everything Works the Same for Everyone

I was born in 1963 to unwed, underage parents. Both my parents quit school, my mother to take care of me, and my father to go off into the Navy. My father told me his side of the story a few years before he passed. He had spoken to his gym teacher about my mom's pregnancy. The teacher suggested he join the military. My mother has never mentioned her experience or what happened between the two of them. My mother was left as an abandoned single parent to deal with the hardships, punitive backlash from her family, and societal implications from unwed teenage parenting. My paternal grandparents were very involved in my life. My dad lived with them, but my memory of him back then is bleak. He was always in his room. My dad returned from the Navy a heroin addict. He lived with his parents, married another woman, and had another child, my half-sister. I learned from my half-sister that when she was seven, her mom left her behind, telling her she was going to the store, and never returned. She was shot and killed.

My mom met my stepdad when I was seven. Things then became more upbeat. It was a turn toward a new season, a new vibe, a new era. In those days, brown, orange, and green plaids and wooden arm living room home furnishings were popular. It was when the high-fi stacked-stereo system: receiver, turntable or CD player, tape deck and big, tall speakers made their debut from the modernized Magnavox midcentury modern stereo turntable consoles. My stepdad brought us soul music, laughter, fun, engagement with unfamiliar new family members, and outdoors BBQs where I was encouraged to entertain the family by singing Michael Jackson's song "ABC," dance to James Brown's songs; get up and do the funky chicken dance, and sing at the top of my lungs, mimicking Diana Ross and Aretha Franklin. The first couple of years of having my new stepdad were emotionally charged, musically inclined, energetic, and exuberant.

I got through elementary school just fine through the long winter months. I stayed inside the house looking outside through the window during hot summer days because what went on behind closed doors was not to be talked about. I was a talker. But then junior high school happened; I discovered what I could get away with, including smoking cigarettes, skipping school, and catching the bus downtown to steal myself cool outfits to sneak to school to wear there. By then, I had outgrown my mom's pin-the-pattern-to-the-material, homemade, sewn clothes. My mom worked every day. My stepdad hustled money on the streets and mostly used it for his pleasures: drinking and drugging. These activities left my mom providing for the family. She didn't miss a day of work; the bills had to get paid. I was left alone to figure out on my own adolescent developmental stage. I had been introduced to hot wine to relieve the pain from ovulating. Nobody took it upon themselves to talk to me about the birds and the bees. I learned everything I needed to know by skipping junior high school with my boyfriend. When I graduated from junior high, I never saw that boyfriend again.

High school became important to me only because I had a junior high counselor who took it upon herself to take me aside privately after the school principal had a run-in with my mother. I had gotten called on the carpet for missing so many days of school. The principal called my mom in to talk. By the time my mom left the school that day, the principal was all over every move I made. He let me know, point blank, I was a troubled child. He impressed upon me that I needed to speak with my counselor, and he made me an appointment during school hours. I had to leave class to see her once a week for the last six months before eighth grade graduation. She told me I was an intelligent young lady and she wanted to help me. She showed me my grades from the times when I did attend school, and she offered to help me choose a high school outside of my school district, not the local high school. She thought I would benefit by going to a high school on the opposite side of town, the West Side, where I would have an opportunity to sign up for a program that, if I kept my grades up, would set me up for success. At that time, I would go to school half a day and work the other half. She encouraged me to come to school every day until graduation so she could sign me up for the program. I followed her directions. Whatever happened the day my mom spoke with the principal, it seemed to me that my principal, counselor, and teachers decided to step in without my mom's permission, to guide me. I showed up like they asked me to. I did what they asked me to do, and I started to take a liking to school. My counselor gave me an award certificate when I graduated. It made me feel proud of myself.

Meanwhile, things at home were getting worse. The fighting between my mom and stepdad became far more frequent. I started biting my fingernails. I frequently snuck hot wine to calm my nerves and help me sleep through the night instead of waking up to my mom's crying or my stepdad's yelling. Catching the bus from the East Side to the West Side was not always the most fun during the winter months. I had to wake up while it was still dark out to walk three blocks to the bus stop, sometimes through four or five inches of snow.

Somehow, my mom agreed that I could attend high school on the West Side of town. Normally, I was told "no" whenever I had an opportunity to do something I wanted. But this one time, my counselor got her to agree. Then I figured out how to create more freedoms for myself. Instead of coming straight home from school and feeling imprisoned by looking out the window, I lied about how long it took to get home on the bus. I carved out some time and space for me to hang out, sometimes with friends, but usually by myself. I would often walk through downtown and go into Woolworth's or Hudson's. Hudson's was a large department store chain that first originated in Detroit's historical opera house building. I spent hours exploring there before I would catch a bus home. My mom was off work by five, so I knew to be home by then or the consequences would be heavy.

A few weeks into catching the bus to the West Side, I discovered a group from my neighborhood met up at one specific bus stop on the corner of Kercheval and Concord. We all went to the same high school. I left my house at a certain time to meet up with them every morning. We all became good friends. We looked for each other every day. If one of us were missing, we'd ask the others where they were. If one of us were running late and we saw them running toward the bus stop, we blocked the doors so the bus driver couldn't close it until that person got on the bus. Once we got on the bus, we entertained each other. We had a long bus ride. Some of us told jokes, some of us sang our favorite Motown songs, and others showed off their talent with musical instruments. We bonded tightly over our freshman year. We never missed a day of school. We made a fuss on the bus that was too much fun to miss.

One of the first days of my sophomore year, one young man, a freshman, caught my attention. As we all maintained our bus stop meeting routine, a few freshmen joined us. This one young man started serenading me. He brought his guitar on the bus and played beautifully for us all while he stared at me. It didn't take long for us to meet up after school and find places to hang out to have sex. And it didn't take long for me to find out what missing a period was about. I didn't mention to anyone that I had missed my monthly mainly because I didn't pay attention. I was busy having fun, going to school every day, meeting up with different friends, discovering new places to hang out and new friends' houses to visit, spreading my wings and learning more about my city of Detroit.

Sometimes, I snuck my boyfriend into my house to have sex. Nobody was home until 5 p.m. However, one time my stepdad came home early. He heard us scrambling to hide. I was trying to stuff my guy into the closet. My stepdad came to the back of the house where we were and heard the noise in the closet. We were busted. My guy came out of the closet and my stepdad talked to us. He never told my mom. He knew it would not go well for me. He just wanted to be the cool stepdad, so I thought. Four months later, my mom discovered I had been missing my monthly. Sure enough, I was pregnant, going from my sophomore year into my junior year of high school.

My mom told me to quit school and take care of my child like she'd had to quit school to take care of me. Rebelliously, I did not. Not everything works the same for everyone.

Quitting school for me just was not an option. School was my only outlet from my emotional pain—pain stored from birth. The physical pain and the emotional battery I endured from time to time had settled in deeply. The sadness, loneliness, and despair I experienced many days behind closed doors warped my sense of self. I was tired of waking up in the middle of the night listening to the sounds of things crashing to the ground, the poundings on the wall, the name calling, and my mom and stepdad's constant fighting. I knew I didn't want to sit around at home, plus school was where my friends were. I had created a tight bond with many friends, and losing them would crush my world. I thought about the opportunity I had signed up for. I envisioned that completing this high school was my way out and my only option. Even though my mom said everything she could to shame me, I wasn't ready to give up the connections I had established, pregnant or not. I thought long and hard and told myself, "I am not my mother."

I took the initiative to speak with my high school counselor. I figured since my junior high counselor was helpful, maybe I should take my chances and talk my situation over with my new counselor. Through my counselor, I found out the high school had daycare. It was a class for students who were going into healthcare or a similar program. And it happened. I decided with my counselor to be out of school exactly six weeks. I got my homework assignments and turned them all in. The school prepared to be my support. I signed up for childcare, with the condition that I show up to school and do my best. I caught the bus every single day in four or five inches of snow during the winter, and my friends who met me at the bus stop helped me carry my newborn to get on the bus. They helped me tote her around in her carry all, and they made sure I had a seat on that bus every day. My teachers watched me as I showed up to school every single day. I saw them side-eyeing me and talking among themselves in the halls. But school was one of my outlets, so I stuck with it.

I did find other outlets to release my pain and carry me through. Drugs was one outlet; alcohol was another. I started drinking at age eleven. I now know drinking at such a young age contributes to alcoholism. The adults in my life decided that giving me some hot wine was a solution for stomach pain. Those were old remedies passed down from one generation to the next. But those remedies did not work well for me the way they worked for other family members. I began searching for the hot wine every chance I got. I learned that hot wine not only buried my physical pain, but it buried my emotional pain. I transitioned from seeking hot wine to smoking cigarettes and smoking pot all through high school. I advanced to smoking crack right after I graduated from high school. I was on the road to experiencing things I never could have imagined. Two things were significant: I didn't quit because I had my child, and I graduated from high school, something my mother hadn't had an opportunity to do. Not everything works the same for everyone.

My Personal Pursuit of Happiness

Almost everything seemed unfair and unjust when I was growing up. I experienced quite a few significant events. One situation I recall vividly was being in a narrow hall, walking up red, carpeted stairs. The adults were yelling and screaming, and someone was crying. Things felt chaotic and disturbing, but I didn't know what was going on. Finally, I got to the top of the stairs and...and this person just grabbed me by my coat collar and carried me through the house with my feet dangling in the air. He threw me on the bed and pulled my underwear down. He rubbed himself on me.

Suddenly, I felt like I had wet myself, but I knew I hadn't. He told me to go wipe myself. This incident shook my soul and confused me. I didn't understand what was happening. I just remember feeling like I was the brunt of everyone else's unhappiness. I got mistreated because other people were unhappy, so unhappiness slowly seeped into my soul. I was three years old.

Who remembers the term "That's a damn shame?" I learned it well. For a very long time, I thought it was my name. I heard the term so much I started to live my life like it was a damn shame. At twelve, I was so sad about being a damn shame that I swallowed an entire bottle of aspirin to kill myself. I fainted. My stomach hurt, but I didn't die. I carried on with life, crying about everything at the drop of a pin. Everything seemed painful. Many of my wounds came from intense whippings. One time, my hands were tied behind my back and my legs were tied together, and I got whaled on with an extension cord. I thought my life would end there, but my very small sisters took licks to help untie me.

Days later, I saw my aunt. I said nothing about my experience, but my face wore sadness all the time. One of my aunts told me, "I will be glad when you find some tears of joy." I had no idea what "tears of joy" meant at that time. But I clearly recall, after two years in recovery, I searched out that aunt's phone number. I called and told her that I had finally learned, after all those years, what tears of joy were. I had finally shed some.

My pursuit of happiness took many forms. Going to school every day was one. I was happy to be around people who made me feel alive.

But then the damn shame thing happened again; as mentioned above, I got pregnant at sixteen. After my daughter was born, I was told it was a damn shame that I took my daughter to school with me—they had a daycare program for students with children so we could bring them with us and finish high school. The one thing I was capable of doing was showing up for school. Although I was condemned for doing it, I showed up and did my best to learn. I didn't skip one day of high school. It was way too much fun, especially in my junior and senior years.

I was a high school business student. Shorthand was my favorite subject. I had two teachers who watched me like a hawk. I could feel them talking about me in the hall. They were always looking my way, as if they were taking notes and comparing them. One or the other would greet me outside their classroom door at least once a week. I think they conspired to encourage me. My grades were above average. They knew I brought my infant across the city to school in cold winter temperatures.

I caught that bus; come rain or shine, I was there. We didn't have too many school closures back then. The snow would be five or six inches deep. I would dress in layers of clothes. I'd wrap my baby girl up in bundles of blankets. Off I went, walking two blocks from home to the bus stop. The bus stop was always crowded. My friends and I knew the bus schedule. We had to transfer buses downtown. The morning ride was all about "hurry up and get to school," but the spring weather meant after school was going to be tons of fun.

How did I get by? I hustled marijuana joints. Back then, students liked roll joints to smoke in the school bathrooms. I met a man I bought pot from after school. This guy rolled joints for me and shared the profits with me as pay. It not only supported my pot habit, but it also put dollars in my pocket. After school, I was able to buy myself food. I loved this one place that sold the best corned beef sandwiches. Another favorite place was the popcorn shop. They sold a variety of flavored popcorn. My favorite combination was cheese and caramel. Passing through downtown Detroit was the only way to transfer on the bus line from where I lived to get to the West Side. I do not recall any talk about a north and south side. Detroit has always been divided between the East and West Sides. Living on the East Side of Detroit and going to school on the West Side was challenging. It could have easily turned into a problem for me being an Eastsider coming to school selling joints, but I became popular. Being one of the few females selling joints was unusual in itself, and coming from the East Side meant I had all the more nerve when the business of selling marijuana was known to have been established by boys from the West Side in West Side schools. Upon reflection, I never once thought about any consequences from breaking established street rules. I just did it. For me, a female from the opposing side of town, to establish her own hustle out of necessity took a bit of courage.

Although I prided myself on showing up to class every day, I also met groups of girls in different bathrooms near my classroom at the time to whom I sold my marijuana joints. I thought my pot-selling might be what my teachers were talking about when they stared at me as they stood outside of their classroom doors before class. I'm sure I usually showed up to class with bloodshot eyes and wreaking from a combination of cigarettes and marijuana. But at the time, I was in a state of oblivion.

I didn't have an income, and I certainly didn't get any cash from my parents, so the hustle was real and serious for me. The stunning thing is nobody asked how I was getting along. I was on my own.

One day, I got word someone wanted me to meet them between classes in the bathroom. When I did, someone I didn't see came up behind me and snatched my purse and my sack full of joints. Denounced by some West Side girls, I was set up by them, and they had the backing from the West Side boys. Word got out to the girls who were my regular customers. A few of them confronted one of the girls who set me up. I didn't know I was liked enough to have someone stand up for me, and I didn't know I was caught up in the complexities of the inner-city East Side-West Side war. The girls who did the confronting were from a rougher junior high school than I was. They were gang members and considered me a homegirl. After they stood up for me, threatening a fight as serious as the East Side girls against the West Side girls, the West Side girls backed down.

I became a strong presence in school. The boys from the West Side started respecting, protecting, and flirting with me. I felt confident. On one hand, with their support, I was inspired to do more and felt a part of a larger community. On the other hand, I also competed for getting the best grades with the smartest students in the school, and I felt like a strong part of that group. I hung out with the smartest group of people, both boys and girls in class. I was really shooting toward my personal goal to make the grade to participate in the program my senior year. It was my reason for being accepted into the school.

My senior year went well. My grades were good enough, and I got into the program. I went to school half of the day and worked the other half. The same two teachers who were always eyeballing me worked together to ensure my enrollment in the program.

I was sent to work for the Internal Revenue Service in the shipping department. Our department shipped out payroll to all of the IRS' other employees throughout the country. I moved out of my mom's and moved into an apartment next door to one of the smartest boys in my class. He drove me to and from school and work every day. We broke up just before prom. Not only was I graduating from high school, but I upped my game and got involved with someone I know now to have been one of the runners to the biggest drug kingpin in Detroit. My character was shaping. Moving one boyfriend out and moving the other one in was part of the lifestyle. The drug kingpin gave us one of the drug ring's fanciest cars, a brand new, two-toned, pink and burgundy Cadillac Seville, for me to attend my prom.

I barely made it to prom. I was too busy riding around, snapping pictures, and showing off the fancy car and my prom dress. I drew my prom dress on a piece of paper. The seamstress took that drawing and sewed my prom dress without a pattern, just from sight, and I showed up to prom in style.

I graduated from high school feeling good, but behaving poorly. I missed being on the honor roll by one low grade, but I was happy. I had done it! I made it through by being involved in both the drug culture on campus and showing up to class and working for my grades. Completing high school was one of the first things I felt proud of. It was part of my pursuit of happiness.

After graduation, I got hired permanently at the IRS. I had to be there at 6 a.m. Six o'clock comes early when you have partied all night.

My drug-dealing boyfriend started bringing the good stuff home. Smoking freebase cocaine was popular at the time. Freebase is cocaine broken down into oil form, which when cooled, forms into a solid substance we called rocks, which were an (almost) pure form of cocaine. Cocaine in its purest form is potent and highly addictive. Risk of overdose is high for abuse of freebase cocaine, along with a myriad of health effects. Somewhere down the line, freebase turned into crack, which is another processing of the cocaine, actually mixed with other highly addictive substances. It didn't take long for me or anyone in my circle to realize, at age eighteen, I was headed down the wrong path—and a long winding road it was, at that.

Sometimes as I reflect, I ask myself, "What happened between when I graduated from high school and now?" I lived my life in an unhappy state of mind for so many years. Did it just happen that one day out of the blue, after many years of researching, that one day I decided to change that state of mind and focus on tangible personal goals? Why couldn't I just stop what I was doing and jump back on the straight and narrow path? I couldn't, no matter how hard I tried.

The Difference Between Wrong and Right

I had few good examples growing up to teach me the difference between right and wrong. Both my father and stepfather were drug users, and I learned some years back that my mother had untreated mental health problems. It was hard to tell which parents/stepparents I was mimicking. But the lecture was always the same. I was told dozens of times I was just like my dad because I chose to use drugs as my way to cope.

One night when I was a kid, my mom and stepdad got into a big fight. Normally, my siblings and I would get woken up by my mom and be dragged off to a friend's house. It was always that friend who had babysat me and stolen the money out of my piggy bank. To say the least, I was uncomfortable being in somebody else's house, not knowing what was going on.

I worried about what I would do about school. These interruptions turned my life into turmoil. This happened so many times that I finally got tired of being ripped out of bed into chaos all the time. While my parents were yelling and my mom was packing bags so we could run away from home in the middle of the night, I made a decision: I was just not going to do it anymore. I was just not going to go. I decided if I was wrong for making that decision, I didn't want to be right.

I discovered years later that being forced to choose between my parents was unhealthy for me. I discovered in recovery that I had to learn how my choices affected me and the people around me.

Now that I am no longer drinking and drugging my life away, I can make sound decisions about what is right for me. I listen to people's opinions, which remain similar to what I heard when I was younger, but the difference is I can make decisions based on my conscience. Although I still make mistakes, the difference between wrong and right is now far more clear to me.

Lessons Learned

1. Honesty is the best policy. Lies beget more lies. Telling the truth in the long run is always the easiest route. Honesty keeps you straight with friends and family.

2. Choices have consequences. I learned to think about what those consequences might be before I made a final decision.

3. Love and faith are one and the same.

Questions for Reflection

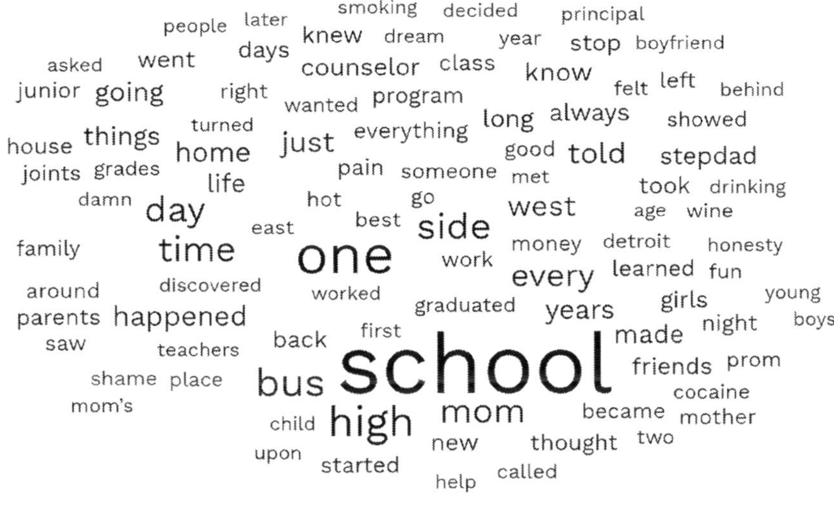

What scary memories do you have from your childhood?

What role did family dysfunction play in those memories?

What did you dream of being or doing when you grew up that was your personal pursuit of happiness?

What was the most difficult lesson in right or wrong that you faced? How did that lesson make you stronger?

____

____

____

____

Chapter 2

Finding People to Support Me

I WOULD NOT HAVE MADE IT THROUGH this life, either before or after I went through recovery, if there had not been special people in my life who valued me and helped me along the way. This chapter is about how I developed some of those relationships.

Live Uncomfortably to Meet the Challenge

Over the years, I've learned there is always a challenge to face. One of my biggest challenges was admitting I needed help. It was difficult to admit I was an alcoholic and drug addict. Where I came from, everyone I knew drank, smoked pot, or did other drugs. It's not a problem when it's a way of life. To admit my way of living was the root of many of my problems was hard to swallow. I kept dragging myself through the gutter so I could keep doing the things I was doing.

Once I admitted to myself that I wasn't living my best life, I gave up much of it—the drugs, booze, the friends—

and made way for geographical moves. While giving up all those things, I discovered I was uncomfortable. I felt lost and indecisive. Every situation and circumstance was brand new for me to deal with. Every skewed emotion and hurt feeling was painful and dogged my every step.

In the beginning, I would go to Twelve-Step meetings and blurt out exactly how I felt with no filter. People at the meetings would laugh quite a bit at what I blurted out. I was as serious as a heart attack in what I said. I expressed every emotion and feeling I had in that moment. I did not understand why what I said was funny to others until a couple of years into recovery when I realized everyone laughed because they understood exactly how I felt. They understood all my thoughts. They related to my behavior.

I lived in that uncomfortable state of being for nearly a year before the relief came. But I clearly understood I had to live uncomfortably to meet the challenge. Today, I fit in my skin. I went through all those emotional days, all those days of darkness, all the while looking at my skewed emotions and my displaced anger. The need to take a good look at what I had developed in my own behavior, my own speech, and my own attitude took a long time to sit with. It was highly uncomfortable.

Normally, I drank to rid myself of discomfort. It took a while to get to stability. I held on to my chair with the whites of my knuckles showing, listening to other people's experiences, like you are listening to mine. I was willing to do the work of self-examination so I could get better the way the people around me in recovery were demonstrating.

I saw some people smiling and laughing; their faces glowed. They didn't seem like they were living in the same negative state of mind I had been living in for all those years. They freely shared their happiness and joy. They shared all their feelings. Of course, I came from a place where you were not supposed to talk about your feelings or show emotions. If you did, you made yourself vulnerable to ridicule, and people would take advantage of you and hurt you.

For so many years, anything I said and felt was used against me. I was called weak for expressing my feelings. I was one big ball of emotions. Finally, I met a group of people who weren't taking the things I said and the things I felt out of context and using them against me. However, some of my family members who have seen my progress still want to carry on the attacks based on the things I did in the past. There is nothing I can do to change that, but for the most part, today, I am comfortable in my own skin.

Just hanging out with people who understood and accepted me for exactly who I am made a huge difference. I felt less judged than I've ever felt before. Don't get me wrong. I really needed the people from my past. I always had people who showed up in my life when I really needed someone. Those people continued to encourage me to keep doing my best until I found the people who taught me how to live—people who are supportive in every way and walk alongside me through tough times.

What Was Given to Me: The Gift of My Aunt

My now eighty-year-old aunt, Lee, who lives in California, was one of the few people who appeared in my childhood and made a lifelong impression. She said kind things. Although I was a little person, she touched my humanity. I was attracted to her like a bee to honey. I was about age five when we first met. The family had talked about her upcoming visit. It was a big deal. I was incredibly snoopy at five. I listened to everything the adults said, even when they didn't think I was listening.

When Aunt Lee finally arrived from California, she was stunning. Her hair was thick, dark, and hung down her back. I measured it with my eyes. It hung down almost to her booty.

She had a caramel complexion with smooth pink lips, glossy and shiny. Her eyeglasses didn't hide her soft brown eyes. I looked at her and thought, *She is the same as me*. It was important to me that we had the same complexion. I was always searching for people I could relate to and connect with. I had a family member tell me once that I came out of the oven just right. My complexion is considered just right, not too dark and not too light. With that idea in mind, I felt an immediate connection to my aunt. There were times when I felt like I belonged to nobody. To finally meet somebody you might belong to was reassuring.

Aunt Lee's voice was like music to my ears. Her grace could not be ignored. She was thoughtful enough to bring me a gift all the way from California. How did she know about me? I had never met her before. I had only heard talk of her. My young mind was intrigued. The gift was a Donald Duck radio. I was highly impressed to receive a gift as popular as one with a Disney cartoon character on it. It was a big deal, and it made me feel like I mattered. Aunt Lee made me feel good about myself. I felt like I had been seen and not just looked at as a burden on a daily basis. I took good care of that radio for many months, a long time to a kid. Paint accidentally scraped off it, but I polished and nurtured that radio every day. Because my aunt treated me kindly, I kept up with her once I got old enough to. When she moved and changed her phone number, I would find out where she moved to and find her number. She teases me about that all the time now. She says, "Child, I would hear my phone ringing and wonder who it was, and it turned out to be you. It tickled me so much that no matter where I moved to or what I changed my number to, you would find me. I always loved that about you." My heart burst into Fourth of July fireworks when I heard those words from her. I have no words to describe how much she meant to me, beginning with that one kind gesture the first time I met her.

I recently drove south on I-5 to see my aunt. We didn't plan to meet since we're living in the middle of the 2020-2021 coronavirus pandemic. One for the record. I called her to let her know I was heading her way. The plan was to call to say hello and wave as I passed her exit. Because the pandemic required strict visiting rules, we had previously talked about not seeing each other. But things quickly changed.

As I approached closer to her town, I called and said, "Auntie, I'm almost near your town. I told you I'm going to call and wave as I drive by." Her voice was softer and quieter than usual. She said, "I was feeling mighty bad about myself before you called. I just wasn't feeling good. And guess who had you call? God had you call." I immediately replied, "Auntie, I'm stopping by to see ya." She came out to meet me at my car in the parking lot of her senior housing complex with a huge smile and carrying a small bag of stuff, a care package. I said, "Auntie, please don't tell me you have a bag of stuff from out of your house to give to me." Sure enough, my aunt had gone around her small, cozy, one-bedroom bungalow and gathered many of her well-kept dainty knick-knacks to gift me. She hasn't changed a bit.

Auntie Lee had all kinds of things in the bag, including jewelry, copies of *The Watchtower* magazine, and napkins. I even got a novel little bitty tube of Chapstick. I mean everything she gave me was stuff she had collected from her secondhand General Store collection, but she's always made me feel special. She said, "I only do that for you." I'm sure she does the same for everyone else, but still, it rekindled in me that relationship from when I was young and she came from California and handed me the Donald Duck radio. I don't know what I've shown her, but hopefully, she sees in my eyes and the windows of my soul that I really appreciate her a lot, because I do.

My aunt often tells me the story she remembers most. She had moved back to Detroit for a short period. She lived next door to my mom's house in her mom's, my grandmother's, house. I had been on one of my visits there. I walked up the backstairs. The back door was open, but the screen door was locked. I knocked to get her attention. She wandered from a room in the front of the house. Before she unlocked the screen door, I said, "Auntie, can I talk to you?" She was trying to open the door. I said, "No, Auntie, I'm not coming in because I've been smoking crack, and I don't want to steal anything from you." My auntie repeats that story to me every single time she sees me. She told me that because I told her the truth about myself, she falls in love with me over and over. She says she prayed to God after I left her door that day. She said she thought about it deeply and then told me, "There's nothing in here you can take; come on in." But I said, "No, Auntie. If you have something for me, I'll take it. But I don't want to come in because I don't want to steal from you." She was a big deal to me even when I was on drugs. I wanted to continue to respect and love my auntie because she was so kind to me all my life, way back when and still now.

What Was Given to Me: My Lifelong Best Friend, Margie, and Her Mom, Jeanette

I discovered many of my high school teachers took an interest in me in different ways, mainly because I showed up to school every day. They knew I had a daughter I was bringing to school with me. I don't know if they knew I was smoking pot and selling joints between classes. But I was glad to be there. There was never a dull moment between learning something new in class and the drama around the school campus.

During this time, strangers showed up in my life. That is how I met my best friend, Margie. We were fourteen. Because Margie befriended me, I had fewer enemies in the school.

One day, Margie came to my house. For the first time, I was allowed to have an outside visitor. I had never before had a friend over for company. Perhaps, I just never asked if I could have a visitor. I was never comfortable enough to know what might happen if I brought someone home. I can't remember if Margie decided to come over on her own volition. Either way, we decided to cook dinner together. We made cooking our project for the day. Somehow or other, I was given permission—I was shocked, but my mom let us take over the kitchen. We stirred up the pots and pans, got water boiling, and prepared a pan of cooking grease. We decided hot-water cornbread, cabbage greens, and fried chicken were the dinner menu items for the day. We rolled our sleeves, washed our hands, and cleaned the cooking area, then mixed and stirred our ingredients. Once we got done, the kitchen was a mess—mixing bowls, pots, and pans were everywhere—but the food turned out tastier than I would have imagined. We served plates to those who were brave enough to taste it. We ate our dinner and felt quite proud of ourselves. To this day, Margie and I still talk about our debut cooking experience.

During Margie's first visit to my house—I recall it vividly—she witnessed something I am not proud of. The family was summoned to go out looking for my stepdad. He had taken the only family car. His disappearing with the car was a regular ordeal. Margie ended up walking the streets with us. My stepdad frequently took off gallivanting around the community while doing drugs with the people in the neighborhood.

We found the car. My mom decided it was a good idea to shoot the car, or shall I say, she decided I should shoot the car. She put the gun in my hands to shoot the car to make it blow up. I took aim and shot at the gas tank. Nothing happened. The car didn't blow up. Margie blurted out, "You've been watching too much TV if you believe the car will blow up with one shot to the gas tank." Margie and I laugh about it now, but in the moment, it felt quite intense. Then it started to rain. Margie gestured to us all, standing out there in the rain, that maybe we should just go home and get out of the rain.

Ever since that day, Margie kept inviting me to her house to meet her mom and family. I had been sheltered in the house during hot summer days and after school. I was too embarrassed to say I couldn't go, so I kept refusing. Margie kept after me until, finally, one day I asked if I could visit her like she had visited me. I had the best time at a backyard BBQ with Margie's family. They extended a kind and warm welcome.

Eventually, I became a disobedient tyrant to my family—at least, that is what I heard on a daily basis. I now know both puberty and the search for my own identity were the root causes of my rebellion. I quickly learned what to say and what to do to get out from under my parents' thumbs. When I was old enough to apply for summer jobs, I did. Working every summer contributed to both building my character and developing a sense of personal responsibility, but I also found myself frequenting Margie's house regularly throughout my teenage years. Her mom had us running errands for her while she cooked huge meals for her family: collard greens, mustard greens, green beans, cabbage greens, cornbread, candied yams, fried chicken, mac and cheese, turkey and dressing, mashed potatoes, BBQ ribs, chicken, hot links, corned beef, pot roast, succotash, fried okra, fried catfish—you name a Southern cooked dish, and she cooked it and we had it, every Sunday. I was adopted into the family, and I rarely missed Sunday dinner.

Margie's mom, Jeanette, was one of the most loving people I ever met outside of my aunt and my favorite grandmother. I clung to her skirt-tail, and she let me. She owned a beauty shop and started doing my hair—no more hot combs over the stove for me. Jeanette told me not to comb my hair, and that's how our relationship started. I had one last of my mom's hot-comb jobs, with the ear scars and neck burn to prove it, before I ended up in Jeanette's chair.

Jeanette was more than just my best friend's mom. She was kind and offered to style my hair weekly. The regular hairstyling morphed into a beauty shop job. Not only did she style my hair, but she taught me how to wash heads, fed me lunch, and paid me to help her in the shop on Saturdays.

Once I moved out on my own at age sixteen, I spent every holiday at her house. Jeanette always made a big, fancy meal. She owned a pool table and kept it in in her neatly remodeled basement. One year on my birthday, Jeanette covered that entire pool table with Southern-cooked dishes. No one had ever cooked a meal like that to celebrate me before. I had never felt so loved! This woman pushed me, nurtured me, and encouraged me to be the best person I could be.

Margie's mother purchased her a brand-new car right off the assembly line for her graduation gift. The first thing we decided to do was take a nice long road trip. We got in her brand-new Ford Mustang, an impressive car for a seventeen-year-old, and decided to head to New York. We were first-time road trippers, without family; fresh graduates free to roam. We smoked a pile of pot that entire road trip. I was so high the clouds started forming into vivid, moving pictures. The faster we drove and the more miles we covered, the more the clouds created in my mind a cute, long-eared puppy with his tongue hanging out of his mouth who was running across the sky. Margie proclaimed me to be her wild, adventurous buddy after that. Our second attempt at a wild experience was a charm for her. She had previously coerced me to wear shorts under our graduation gowns on graduation day. She knew I had no adult supervision directing me otherwise. I lived on my own in an apartment at the time. Embarrassingly so, I was the only one from the group who discussed wearing shorts who actually wore them. She later told me that although she had tried to get away with wearing shorts, her mom would not allow her out without wearing proper attire. Self-consciousness washed over me, but immediately, I wiped that self-awareness expression off my complexion, turned my attention toward the most important life accomplishment I'd ever had, and proudly walked across that stage.

Unfortunately, not long after graduation, my life spun out of control. Although I was held hostage to cocaine by then, Margie and I hung together like wet clothes. Months after she moved out on her own, she decided we should throw our very first party—an unforgettable party to say the least. We made our own rules, including bring your own booze (BYOB). Our bar of booze was stacked with good expensive drink, like Cardon Bleu Cognac. We, of course, had our regular favorites: Boone's Farm Strawberry Hill, wine coolers of all flavors, and Heineken beer. The highlight of the party was the movie Margie chose. It was of the educational variety. I had never heard of it, but she said it was good. She knew I was up to trying new things. Although she'd always blamed the bad stuff on me, she'd always been an influence. We popped popcorn, drank our drinks, smoked our pot, and popped in the VHS player the perverted, Rated X version of the rise and fall of the notorious Roman Emperor Caligula, which included hardcore gay and straight orgy scenes and a few explicit lesbian oral, unsimulated masturbation, and penetration sex scenes. I still question if that was the night she conceived her only child.

A few years later, we threw another unforgettable party. I had been moved out into a flat in Grosse Pointe Park. The drug kingpins made me the babysitter of the drugs in the attic and the cash in the grill of the floor. I hadn't gone out of the house for months. With my nonstop supply of uncut cocaine, I had no reason to leave and was now hostage to my flat. It made sense to marry the guy who peddled the drugs and turned me out. A party seemed fitting to celebrate my elevated position. Margie and I planned an all-girls party. I insisted the regular free base partying with all the guy visitors, including my uncle and husband, stay out that night. Margie and I rounded up our drinks and our marijuana, and I made a special purchase of mescaline, a psychedelic hallucinogen. Surprisingly, most of the young ladies I invited showed up. I greeted each of them at the door to let them know about the buffet of "get-high." Some of them knew each other, and others met for the first time. As I walked through my flat, assessing the turnout and high out of my mind on the mescaline, I was quite impressed by the way we all engaged with one another, listening to our favorite Motown sounds. A few hours into our get-together, there was a knock on the door. I opened it to the bum-rush of all the guys I had shooed away. They crashed the party. Margie and I reflect on that night and mark it as another successful and fun event, but nothing would surpass our family Halloween party.

In my flat, the drug kingpin left quite a few nice home furnishings. I had a 200-gallon fish tank on the mantle in my living room. The wife of the drug kingpin left my daughter's bedroom plush—pink carpet, a white canopy bed with a matching dresser, and a big Barbie dollhouse. Quite cozy, but for our Halloween party, Margie and I upped our game. We decorated the house and moved the furniture to corners. We needed the space for the many kids' games we had planned like pin the tail on the donkey, bobbing for apples, and spinning the kids to make them dizzy. We bought other games for the kids to engage in, and we bought all their prizes. We made tons of finger foods, and we invited tons of people. One of my friends piled in with a few of her sisters and their children. One of my younger sisters and a couple of my cousins showed up and hung out with me that night. Many of the neighbors' lawns were filled with Halloween décor. One neighbor made their house into a haunted house. My flat was so overcrowded that someone nearly knocked down one of my lamps. My oldest daughter was nearly three years old. She was so overwhelmed by the crowd that she followed me through the house, telling me to watch people who were touching our stuff. Out of the blue, the fun family scene ramped up to an extremely chaotic moment. Kids and grownups alike were screaming, nearly trampling over each other throughout my place. Someone walked in with one of the ugliest, scariest, and raunchiest smelling Halloween costumes I had ever seen. He came in limping, with ripped blood-stained clothes and laughing wickedly with a twisted stringy wig. I could barely see through the crowd that was bunched up in corners of the kitchen and dining room. But then I learned this scary person had locked himself in the bathroom with my daughter and a few other kids. It took me a good long five minutes to worm my way through everyone. Margie and I met up at the same time. Not only did she have my back again, but she literally stood behind this person's back, ready to take action as I prepared to take him down from the front. Laughing hysterically, at that moment he somehow knew to take off his mask. It was Margie's boyfriend. The tension subsided with our sighs of relief. He was so tickled that his long-awaited secret plan to crash the Halloween party had come off better than he had planned.

Our fresh-out-of-school years were fun for both Margie and me, but then my years became rocky. I had transitioned from my parents' domestic violence to my own drug-induced violence. Years of fighting between my parents continued, and my mom was still running off, now with my sisters and to my place. One night while my mom was there, my husband came home and decided to slap me out of a chair. I got up and whaled on his ass. We rolled against the walls, punching each other. My mom sat on my living room couch silent, not budging, but watching us fight. He ended up running out of the door and down the stairs to get away from me. In disgust, I turned toward my mother. I flashed back to the time she had told me, right after she had been beaten by my stepfather, to "wait until it happens to you." After hearing that come from my own mother's mouth, I had vowed never to allow a man to put his hands on me and get away with it. I faced her and blurted out, "You sat here, let him put hands on me, and didn't intervene—you allowed this man to put his hands on your daughter. Get out!" She remained silent as

I watched her pack up my sisters and their things and leave. I was beyond hurt.

Days later, Margie came over to help me pack up my things so I could leave the situation. She watched as I threw furniture off the balcony to get away. She nearly broke her toe helping me. I managed to make it out alive; however, I was now more vulnerable to my addiction. I struggled to get clean. I stayed clean long enough to meet a new boyfriend who worked at a parking garage in downtown Detroit. I stayed clean long enough to get hired for a few jobs too: at Michigan Consolidated (Mich-C on), the gas company in Detroit where I stayed for a couple of years; a temporary position at Edison, the light company in Detroit, which lasted about six months; and the car-rental where Margie worked, where I was also for almost a couple of years.

Becoming a part of Margie and Jeanette's family was the beginning of what would be given to me. When Jeanette found out I was pregnant at nineteen with a second child, she fussed over me every time she saw me. I ended up having my second child on her birthday. I saw pure joy in her eyes when my son was born. Although I was not her family member by blood, her family all showed up for me. We have shared watching our children and our children's children grow up over the years. Although Jeanette was fussy at times about the troubles she saw me heading toward, she was the mom I had always wished I'd had. She always considered what I liked. She always took good care of my hair, and she helped my emotional healing by listening and just being there for me. I didn't feel judged; I just felt wrapped in a blanket of love.

What Was Given to Me: My Grandmother

My paternal grandmother was the most important person in my life and the best grandmother a girl could ask for. I adored her. I didn't think anyone in the world loved me as much as she did. I mean, she was just an average woman who did house cleaning for the people who owned Stroh's Ice Cream. I was about six or seven when she took me to work with her. Her goal to teach me how to make beds went by the wayside once I got there. The house was a mini-mansion. I went from room to room in these people's house. I'll never forget wanting to play with every stuffed teddy bear and all the kids' other toys.

Of course, the people who owned the house were white. My grandmother was a cleaner who got in the car with a bunch of black women and drove for what seemed like forever to get to the places where they cleaned and worked. This was 1969 or 1970.

Granny used to give me all the Stroh family's hand-me-downs. I remember thinking, *Oh, how wonderful she is. I'm wearing these sexy Fifth Avenue-like gowns.* I had all these name brand clothes.

My grandmother was something special to me. I'm sure you have a grandmother or someone special in your life whom you know without a doubt loves you unconditionally. When I was born out of wedlock, my grandmother and my grandfather decided to be there for me because my father took off.

The Universe Returns What You Put Out Into It

When I was born, my grandma was there. When she took her last breath, I was there. I always loved going to my grandma's house. Her house was aromatherapy. It always smelled like baked 7-Up cake. She cooked dinner nearly every day, even after having a stroke that left her paralyzed. I watched her stand with her wheelchair behind her to help her balance and to catch her if she fell. She stood at her kitchen sink for hours washing her greens, leaf by leaf, with the one hand she could still use, making sure no worms or bugs of any kind made it into her pot of home-grown, cooked collard greens.

Granny had rules in her house. Everyone in the house followed her rules during breakfast and dinner. She set the table, one way for breakfast and another way for dinner. It was so routine that even guests abided by her rules. We all had to sit at the table for breakfast and dinner, and Granny cooked our favorite meals. She would ask us what we liked. I remember thinking, *Wow, what do I like? My grandmother's going to cook me what I like!* Granny made us what we liked so we could all come to the table, and coming together at Granny's table was when we shared stories.

My grandmother would laugh and talk about her father. She told me if I had ever met him, I would have loved him much like she did. And then my grandfather would tell his stories about his experience in Aliceville, Alabama, and how he and Granny met and how they got to Detroit. My grandfather's house was his inheritance from his mom. They moved from Aliceville, Alabama. His mom had owned a restaurant so she could afford to buy a home in Detroit. That house is still in the family.

My first job as a teenager was right across the street from my grandmother's house. I wanted to be close by. It was at the community center, which was a popular place back in the day. I was a switchboard operator—the old-fashioned kind—I had to pull a cord, plug it into the switchboard, and push the button to ring a number. It was a fun job, but most of all, it kept me near to my dear grandmother. I was attached to her for life, and she accepted it.

Once I was a teenager, I was very difficult for my parents to handle. My grandmother would spoil me and then send me home. I'm sure that was uncomfortable for all involved.

As I got older and started going astray, my grandmother would pray for me every time I saw her. She was a very religious woman. She read her Bible daily and prayed multiple times a day. It seemed like she had to. And I know she was praying for me all the time because I was always crying unhappy tears.

Once I dove into drugs and alcohol, when I would visit her, Granny would meet me in her wheelchair and check me at the door. I couldn't go past her without her giving me the once over with her eyes. She started at my toes and stopped once she reached the tips of my hair. And then she would ask me, "How are you doing?"

Of course, as things got worse for me, Granny knew the answer just by looking me over. She never said a bad word to me. She never said anything negative. She was always positive. I just adored her so.

Granny was so meticulous. Her windowsills had to be dust free. Her living room, dining room, and kitchen were set like she liked them. Before she ran out of energy as she got older, her house could pass a white glove test any day. Dust was not tolerated. That is how my grandmother cared for us in her home as well. And that's what I took from her and owned as my own. For me, the things she did were significant, loving gestures, and I will wear her kindness like a tattoo across my heart forever.

In 1987, I moved to California. Although we spoke on the phone often, there were many times I missed being in my grandmother's presence. Her abounding love healed. There was never a time I was in town that I did not see her.

In 2005, my grandmother got sick. The doctors checked her colon for cancer. They had her swallow a camera—this was in early 2006. The camera was never recovered, so the doctor decided he would operate to get it out. I was living in California at the time when a family member called saying, "Your grandma wants to see you. She's about to have an operation." I said, "Okay" and flew to Detroit.

My grandmother had her operation. She came home, and less than two weeks later, she was in a hospice bed. I was shocked. The whole family was shocked. Clearly, the surgery didn't go well. But my grandmother lay in her hospice bed in her dining room area. I cried and drank daily out of sorrow and sadness. My grandmother didn't talk. She answered by shaking or nodding her head yes or no. Her stares frightened me; she looked at me long and hard. When I moved, her eyes moved with me—it was her way of connecting with me, even on her deathbed, a sign. I knew my grandmother loved me so, and she knew I loved her, too.

Between my aunts and uncles, everyone was in charge of some task for her, except me. I was the oldest grandchild, so I demanded to be recognized and in charge of something, but nobody trusted me. Why should they? I was irresponsible. I mean, I was behaving quite erratically, sneaking in and out of the side door at all hours of the day and night. The door squealed and told on me every time. Hospice brought Granny oxygen, and one of my aunts decided to allow me to be in charge of the machine. I had figured out how it worked for her, so she deemed me capable.

Soon after, I was out partying. When I came to out of my trance from heavy drugging, it dawned on me that I had forgotten to give my grandmother her oxygen. I jumped straight into my gym shoes and ran down the dark, dreary, scary streets of Detroit at 4:00 a.m. I ran non-stop for six blocks, all the way to my grandmother's. I got there and realized I had left my key back at the place I had just left. Without knowing the time, I banged on the back door. I yelled, but not too loudly, hoping someone would hear me and let me in. I repeated over and over as I banged, "I forgot to give grandmother her oxygen." It took a few minutes, but my auntie opened the door and said, "Girl, where's your key?" I said, "I forgot it. But I really wanted to come and give grandma her oxygen." My aunt said, "You know, nobody's been down here with your grandmother all night. Let me go in and check on her."

My aunt went in and checked on Granny. Something forced me to walk past the room and go sit on the stairs. I sat on those stairs waiting for the okay to go in, but what I heard was, "Oh, my God, she's not breathing."

Something took me out of myself right then and there. I had an out-of-body experience. I went into a zone where everything was done and said in slow motion. My grandfather came running down the stairs. He stepped over me to get past. As he made his way as fast as he could with his artificial leg, he asked me what had happened. But he just kept right on going past me without waiting for a reply.

My hearing became super-sensitive, bionic almost. I heard every word uttered by everyone in the other room. The phone rang right in the midst of the chaos, crying, and wailing. I heard my grandfather pick it up and say, "Hello, who is this?" The next words that came out of his mouth were, "You killed my wife." He slammed the phone down on the receiver so hard I was sure it was broken. "Timely call," is all I could manage to whisper to myself as I sat there for hours upon hours.

I sat there long enough to watch the EMTs arrive to take my grandmother out on a stretcher. I sat there long enough to watch family members come and go. Everyone walked past me as if I were not even there. In many ways, I wasn't.

My family had mistrusted doctors since my grandfather's leg had been amputated in 1940 following a car accident. Then my grandmother's operation wasn't successful at all. I sat on the stairs thinking to myself, *I can't trust the doctors. I can't trust the world I'm in anymore.* The one person who made me feel secure in the world, the only person in my family who gave me unconditional love, was gone. I sat there thinking, *Why am I breathing right now?*

I went through that stage of grief for over a year. My grandmother passed in July of 2006, days short of her and my grandfather's sixty-third wedding anniversary. After my grandmother's funeral, I walked the streets until I wore holes in the soles of my shoes. Later, I heard that some of my family had searched the streets for me. They had feared I was dead. Sometimes, I showed up for a meal, but other times, I showed up because I was plain old tired. I hoped walking it out would help ease the pain. I was so lost and so sad. I thought I should die.

Love Conquers Everything

For months after my grandmother died, I would have flashbacks to how my grandmother looked at me before her death and how I felt like she was trying to send me the message that she knew she was leaving and wanted me to know she loved me. I often reflected on the times when my grandmother had looked at me, starting at my toes all the way up to the tip of my hair to see how I was doing. I reminisce about the times she would dig deep down into her bra and pull out a few dollars for me. I knew she did that so I wouldn't have to be without when I was out there on the streets. My grandparents always made sure I had something to eat and some place to sleep when nobody else would have me. I remembered my grandmother praying for me in my presence. Her love sustained me through all those days of darkness. It turns out that my recovery celebration date is one day after my grandmother's birthday. I have been in recovery in honor of her ever since.

Somehow, God allowed Granny to continuously be a significant force in my life. Her love sustained me and carried me through plenty of down days. At least I have her to remember. My grandmother was special. Later, I discovered she was not just special to her family. Other people talk fondly about her, too. She touched hearts. As time passed, I heard others' stories of how special she was to so many people. I had no clue, but I do now.

I bet you have that one person whom you know loves you unconditionally. And so, today, I hope you not only carry that in your heart, but you pass unconditional love on to the people around you because my grandmother told me one thing that I know is true today: loves conquers everything!

My Grandfather

I had always liked sitting across the table from my grandfather to listen to his stories. When he told the story of losing his leg, I peered into his eyes, which were watery. He recounted his tale of how it had happened when he was a teenager. My grandfather and his cousins were walking down the road, an old country road without sidewalks or streetlights, when a car hit him so hard it knocked him into the ditch. The car stopped, and the young man got out and picked up Grandpa. He put Grandpa in his car and drove him to the local hospital. At the hospital, the doctor sat Grandpa in a room, walked out, and basically forgot about him. Instead, the doctor went to talk to the gentlemen who had hit Grandpa to ask him if he was okay. "Are you in trouble? Will you be okay?"

My grandfather sat in that room for so many hours, long enough for gangrene to set in. When the doctor came back to finally check on my grandfather, he did the surgery right there. As he told the story, my grandfather said, "All I could hear was the sound of my bones clinking in that tin garbage can."

My grandfather's leg was amputated. It was the year before the United States entered World War II. My grandfather sat on the porch with one leg, wishing he could go off to war with all the other young men. He was only eighteen, a young man sitting in despair over something that could have been prevented. The young man who took my grandfather to the hospital was a young white boy who intended to help my grandfather. That young man took my grandfather to a hospital where the doctor was an old white man who was practicing exactly what doctors practiced in 1940. The lack of services rendered to my grandfather was simply due to the color of his skin, a black man living in the American South.

Another time, my grandfather told me about the time he was running through town when suddenly this rope wrapped around his body. An old white snake oil salesman had decided to use my grandfather as an example. He was only nine. "I wiggled and wiggled until I got my body loose enough to remove that whip. Once I got loose, I ran and ran and leaped over this very tall fence to get away. I often reflect on how frisk of a young lad I once was. I sat on my front porch dispirited day after day watching other young folk *walk* past."

His mother, my great-grandmother, owned a restaurant, so eventually, she was able to afford to buy him a prosthetic leg.

My grandfather was a funny man. I got to know him and enjoy his humor by sitting at the dinner table with him. I often wish I had written down all the funny things he said and sent them to the local newspaper. I never did. But his humor left a lifelong impression on me. Mainly because he usually was such a serious man.

My grandfather lived through many years of deep emotional pain, working hard for his family as an elevator operator while earning scraping-at-the-bottom-of-the-barrel wages. He told me how he had no choice but to feed his family beans every day. But saving money was important to him. He did not spend frivolously. He was so tight with money that there was an old family saying that he squeezed tears from George Washington's eyes on the dollar bill. He saved his money like no other person I have known. Once he retired, he paid cash for his Cadillac. He had made up his mind that was the way to do it. No credit for him. He taught me how to read each line on all the utility bills, too. The thermostat was kept at one temperature no matter how cold it was outside. If his bill changed, he read each line to discover why. I had no choice but to learn how to read each line on every bill after he kept busting me for making long distant phone calls from his number.

He was always working on home projects. That old house served my granddad and his family well. When he was alive, he kept the house in tip-top shape.

He practically lived in his basement, though. He would go down every night to get ready for bed. He seemed to spend hours upon hours down there. I often wondered what he did down there, but I never found out. Today, we'd call the basement his man cave. Nobody was welcome down there. If my grandmother needed something or wanted him for something, she'd stick her head in the chute to call down for him.

When my grandmother passed, my grandfather and I both had a hard time with it. We found comfort reminiscing about her. Every single day, I'd find my grandfather sitting at his desk. His desk sat at the bottom of the stairs in the corridor to the front door. He'd be staring off into space. I couldn't sneak past him. He'd stop me to tell me what he missed most about my grandmother. He and I did not miss a day. This dance went on for nearly a year.

My grandfather and I finally bonded. Unaware that my grandmother had taken the spotlight for so many years, suddenly something dawned on my grandfather. He said, "Everything in this house belongs to me." I was sitting at the kitchen table for breakfast like always; the rules hadn't changed, but I looked up. He was staring at me. I knew right then and there that he finally approved of me, and I was included in his world. It was a warm and fuzzy moment, but then he focused his attention on me. My sneaking in and out of the house had become obvious to him—I wasn't good at being sneaky. Not with my grandfather around. And he rarely left the house. I almost held my breath, waiting for moments to be sneaky.

Before my grandmother died, my grandparents had had a routine. I knew what time I could get away with what. That changed significantly now. Every corner I turned, my grandfather was right there. He knew I was misbehaving, doing drugs. One day he asked, "When are you going to be good?" I replied, "Grandfather, I want to be good. I just don't know how."

I now believed my grandfather was praying for me like my grandmother had always done. Nearing my last stretch of partying, I would lie in bed for days, wishing and hoping to fall asleep and never wake up—but I always woke up. I stayed in that room so many days that my grandfather finally bust open the door. He said, "What is wrong with you?"

I honestly did not know what was wrong. He ordered me to the kitchen table. That's where our talks took place. I couldn't talk for crying. I spent days like that. One day, I had gotten myself a beer and was sitting on the porch bawling for no reason at all. He came out, looked at me, and yelled back into the house to my aunt, asking her why she had beat me up and sent me outside. He was trying to get a laugh out of me, but I couldn't laugh.

My journey to recovery began less than a month later.

I ran away to an inpatient center. I didn't tell anyone. I learned later my family searched the streets for me, thinking I had been killed. Honestly, I thought nothing of being inconsiderate.

My grandfather passed in January 2009, three years after my grandmother. With one year of recovery under my belt, I flew back to Detroit. My grandfather then saw me differently. Our talks moved to the living room. This was a statement. Since I was the oldest grandchild and close to my grandmother, he let me in on making the funeral arrangements for her, but this time, the talk was about him. He told me he frequently visited the plot where my grandmother is buried, but his last visit had him perplexed. Someone had placed his name on the plot site. and this was the first time he'd seen it. I rudely interrupted with what I considered a funny comment, but I later discovered it was not. I said, "Grandfather, you are living in the Twilight Zone." Then I sang the music from the TV show.

He continued on with his speech. Since this was the first time he'd seen his name placed there, he sat around thinking about what that meant to him. He divulged to me that he'd been living with prostate cancer for more than twenty-one years. He didn't trust doctors, not after losing his leg, and especially after my grandmother's failed surgery. He admitted he had pain running up his back. He told me he didn't care much about living anymore. He and my grandmother had been married for nearly sixty-three years, and with her gone, nothing mattered in the same way. He told me his wishes and plans for the family house.

I told him how happy I was to visit with him again, and I told him about what I was doing to stay clean and sober. Four months later, my grandfather passed. I said to myself, "If there are angels up above, my grandparents are teaching angels how to love." And most significantly, if my grandfather is with my grandmother, he can share the good news with her that her wishes came true because he had witnessed me as being different—clean and sober.

Lessons Learned

1. Get uncomfortable to get comfortable with you.

2. Do what you can, and look back with no regrets. It was the best you could do at that time.

Questions for Reflection

cooked recovery looked place dinner kind pot although ever car life hair night around loved grandfather back met young quite leg days margie good man even go walked without people years told call mom person love meet aunt running went house detroit grandmother's decided one left felt first made party door later jeanette past sat family let took always changed long things table away time someone moved kept grandmother enough auntie talk sure heard granny hours every old just room day everyone eyes right knew help living know owned home something times nearly special drugs best kitchen finally showed hard

Who are some of the people who have believed in and supported you, especially in your childhood or young adulthood?

____

____

____

____

When has love helped you conquer?

____

____

____

____

What strength have you received or what lessons have you learned from older family members or your family history?

____

____

____

____

What regrets do you have in regards to your family?

____

____

____

____

What can you do to prevent similar regrets in the future?

____

____

____

____

Chapter 3

Leaving Home

It was 1985. I took off for New York with my new boyfriend after leaving my then husband. I had left my kids with my aunt, my mom's youngest sister, for two days. When I got back, family was gathered on the porch, which was weird; something strange was brewing, but I did not know what. There was lots of commotion coming from the porch as I pulled up. I didn't know what had happened or what was said before I got there, but when I got to the gate, chaos broke out. Nothing was clearly spoken. My mom walked toward me swinging a bat. I stopped it by raising my arm, which resulted in a lot of pain. I got my kids and left walking down the street with them. Later that day, I went to the doctor and learned my arm was broken. I spiraled into a deep dark abyss. Day after day, I thought about what had happened, but I couldn't figure it out. It caused me to become physically ill. I caught pneumonia. I lay pathetically in the hospital bed with a cast on my arm and tubes up my nose. I opened my eyes to two people standing at the foot of my bed. One of them was my mom and the other was my sister. Not one word was spoken. I closed my eyes, turned over in disgust, and fell back asleep. The next time I woke up, the room was empty again. It would be ten years before I learned why my mother had hit me. She thought I had stolen her credit card to go out of town, but while I was in the hospital, she found her card, which she had just misplaced. She knew where the card was when she came to visit me, but she never said a word about it. I only learned the truth from my youngest sister when she brought it up one day.

My broken arm mended. I recovered from the pneumonia, but my heart remained shattered. My scarred heart amounted to one huge, repeatedly stabbed gash. Disgust, bitterness, and resentment ruled my world. I could not shake it. I drank more and more to drown my emotions. I managed to get back to work again. This time I was hired on with the IRS at a higher grade from a G-3 to G-4. I was hired as the secretary in the McNamara Building for the department that collected back taxes. Here are a couple of quick stories: I answered the phone like I was trained to. The person on the other end was panting, speaking fast while telling his side of the story. Apparently, an agent had gone out to appraise a house when the person who lived there rushed out, got into their car, and attempted to run the agent down. The agent ran as fast as he could, but he was side-swiped by the car. He said he rushed from the scene to a phone to call my supervisor. I transferred him, but I giggled afterwards and thought to myself, *It's all in a day's work.* Another time, when I answered the phone as usual, the caller calmly said, "I placed a bomb in your building, and I am going to blow it up." I replied calmly, "Can you hold the line one second, sir?" I moved swiftly toward my supervisor's office and shared with him the call I had on hold. When I went back to my phone, the caller was still holding. I calmly told him, "Hold the line one second while I transfer you." My supervisor came out later and shared the conversation with me. The entire office laughed for days about it, but on a serious note, it could very well have been a real threat given the way people felt about the IRS.

I smoked pot before showing up for work. As a result, not only did my coworkers start looking animated as they walked around, but the calls that came in were too. More and more, I started feeling like I didn't fit in. One day, sitting at my desk, the idea popped into my mind that I should just leave Detroit. I had been closely watching and reading quite a few advertisements about the California lifestyle. I daydreamed a lot, but I thought any lifestyle would be better than what I was dealing with here. So, I decided I was moving to California. I left work, went straight to the bank, and withdrew all my cash. I told my boyfriend about my decision and let him know I was going with or without him. That caused a big fuss.

Since he had a job, I didn't want him to just up and leave, but I was not letting anything or anyone stop me. He was at work when I stopped by on my way to the Greyhound bus station. I asked for clarity one last time. He decided at the last second, but not without encouragement from his boss, to just go. He drove me to the Greyhound bus station and waited in the car while I went in and talked with the two people working there, a young man and a young lady. They were busy, but I was relentless. They had given me the price of one-way tickets to Los Angeles, which was more than I could afford; however, I insisted on bargaining. I wouldn't stop following them and telling them how badly I needed to get to California. The young man working with her appeared annoyed by my begging, so he told her to give me the tickets. I ended up convincing the young lady to take my cash and put it in her pocket. She gave me two one-way tickets, one for me and one for my boyfriend. I was both excited and surprised, but now I had two one-way tickets to California, and it had only cost me fifty bucks.

I left my two children behind with a relative until I got settled in. I left with just a few things packed in a carry-on bag. I left behind a messy, fully furnished house. My family hadn't a clue what had happened. I hadn't talked to anyone about my plans. I had no one who could ever understand my thoughts, my pain, or my actions. I left Detroit with the intent never to return. I did return many times for visits, but the visits all had the same result—I drank and drugged myself into oblivion, wishing to blot out all the pain I associated with home, but I couldn't, no matter how hard I tried.

Taking the bus to California was a long, hard, three-day ride. My knees hurt me so much from sitting so long that I could barely walk with my swollen knees. Once I stepped off the bus into the California sun and stood on ground I had yet to explore, I let out the strongest sigh of relief I'd ever had. It was an adventure—starting a life in a place where no one knew me and I, for sure, didn't know anyone. I was determined to make a new beginning somehow, some way.

I got off the bus in downtown Los Angeles. The sun was shining brightly, and the temperature was warm, just like I had imagined California would be. I walked a couple of blocks, asking people where I could find a hotel. I kept running into homeless people. Culture shock—I had never seen people lying on the ground in doorways.

One person asked me where I was from. I told him I had just gotten off the bus from Michigan. He gave me a number to call. I walked a few more blocks, taking mental notes of people pushing all their belongings around in grocery carts. I was both fascinated and shocked by the number of homeless people lined up for blocks on sidewalks while everyone else walked past them. Apparently, this was their norm. Either I was far too naïve or perhaps it was far too cold for homeless people to sleep in doorways in downtown Detroit. I had never seen anything like it.

I continued walking and looking before I decided to stop and use a payphone. The man had given me a number to a shelter in Pasadena. The person on the other end asked me a series of questions. After I answered them all, I got directions. Thus, I was off on my first journey in California, a forty-minute bus ride from Los Angeles to Pasadena.

The bus stop for the shelter let me off right in front of Pasadena City Hall. I was mesmerized by the building's architect. The city streets were clean. There was no trash on the sidewalks, on the curbs, or in the streets like in Detroit. I immediately felt like I had found my place.

I went to the shelter. It was in a church basement. Mattresses were on the floor. My first night in California, I was too tired to be fussy. The rules were that you had to get up by 6 a.m., get out on the streets, and be back by 7 p.m. when dinner was served. Most of the time, there was a long line to get in. If you weren't back by then, you had to stay out all night.

By the second night of my stay, it became apparent to me that most of the people who stayed there were regulars. One guy had dreadlocks. He didn't talk. He always had his banjo strapped to his back. His clothes were ripped and dirty. He never showered. The guy who ran the shelter had been a doctor who became homeless and decided to change his career. I began to see homeless people in a different light. Every night as we all waited to get into the shelter, the guy with the banjo started serenading me. He still never said a word. Others would tell me of places to eat for free within walking distance. I felt like I was building myself a community with these strangers. I felt safe.

My first day in California, I walked through downtown Pasadena, soaking up the sun. I noted the businesses, stores, and uniquely designed buildings. I spotted a temporary employment agency and went in. The woman who worked there, Glenda, met me at the door. She was beautiful and very professional. She asked if she could help me. I explained that I was from Michigan, and I had spent the night in an overnight shelter. I told her I was interested in a temporary job. She sat me down and allowed me to take all the basic tests they used to screen for employment. She later told me she was quite impressed with my scores. I explained that I had worked for the IRS and showed her my badge. Glenda excused herself and went into a back room. When she came back, she asked if I would come back the next day dressed for work. I had two braids, one on each side of my head. I was wearing a jump suit with gym shoes. She also asked if I could bring my badge with me for identification. I agreed. I left there quite satisfied that I had an appointment the next day. I continued to explore and take in the beauty of downtown Pasadena.

The next day, I woke up super-early, showered, pulled my hair back into a bun, and put on a ton of makeup. I pulled out the one dress and one pair of high-heeled dress shoes I had packed. The dress was shiny, silky, and had buttons down the front—a fashion model design. The shoes were beige with three-quarter-inch ankle straps. Knowing my day was going to be long, I put my tennis shoes in my purse. I had a long wait for the agency to open.

At the shelter, breakfast was served upstairs from 6 to 7 a.m. The choice was always oatmeal or cold cereal, fresh fruit, juice, and a pastry. None of those items would have been my choice for breakfast. In Detroit, a normal breakfast included buttered grits and fried pork chops, bacon, eggs, buttermilk biscuits, pancakes, salmon patties, toast, and juice. I didn't even drink coffee at the time. Still, I had to adapt to my circumstances for now. I headed out right after eating.

The moment the agency opened, I walked in. Glenda looked at me twice. She said, "Oh, my, you don't look like the same person who was here yesterday." I showed her my identification. Glenda took it and told me the IRS had told her to send them their property. I couldn't say anything about that, but Glenda seemed genuinely impressed with my appearance. She continued to give me tests, looked up some places I might be interested in working, and gave me some directions. Just before I stepped out the door with directions to a potential temporary job, Glenda slipped me a card with her home address and her personal phone number. She told me if I ever needed anything, while staying at the shelter, not to hesitate to call her.

Ten days of living in the shelter was enough for me. I got into a disagreement with my boyfriend over buying cigarettes or food. My cash was running short. I got fed up and took off from the shelter one evening without my boyfriend. I pulled out the card I had tucked away that Glenda had given me for emergencies. I walked to the address on the card. My courage swelled as I knocked at her door. Talking was one of my best attributes, and I did a lot of it.

Glenda opened her door and invited me in. I started telling her of my journey and what my goals were. I'm not sure which part of my story convinced her to let me stay the night, but she also decided to give me some time to get myself together. A couple of days later, my boyfriend joined me at her house. Six weeks later, we both had full-time jobs and had saved enough to get our own apartment and purchase an old beater car.

Glenda was so impressed with my hard work and accomplishments that she praised me to her coworkers. Eventually, she opened her own temp agency and hired me to help with the office work. With a home, a car, and a job, I sent to Detroit for my two children. My youngest sister brought them, stuck around a couple of years, and babysat while I worked.

I discovered I had been pregnant on the long bus ride to California, which contributed to my swollen knees. I married the boyfriend who came with me from Detroit. We had three children together. I had a set of Irish twins, eleven months apart, and two years later, one more baby boy. I had a total of five children. My family in Detroit learned about all my children and one of my uncles, Uncle Billy, put it to me like this, “I know California grow and produce beautiful things, but would you quit growing and producing so many beautiful things.”

It was a breath of fresh air to have this opportunity for a new start. Nobody really knew me. Although I kept meeting people, I remained isolated most of the time. My husband became a truck driver. With free time and being home alone after work, I decided to venture out. I ventured out and found my drugs of choice, both marijuana and crack. Being a new girl to town, I had no problem telling my story to the neighborhood drug dealers to get them to trust I wasn’t DA.

Thanks to my husband’s truck-driving job, we moved from a rinky-dink apartment to a huge house. Our backyard sloped down to the next street, making our house look like a house on the hill. Our living room was so big, with open space, that I started shopping for grand pianos. I never bought one, but I was in love with the idea. My kitchen windows had no curtains or blinds. They were sun windows. I explored different flowers and plants and planted them all around the windowsill. My husband would bring his truck home and back it into our long driveway. He parked the trailer to cover the kitchen windows; that way no one could see in.

With five kids, time on my hands, and an increased income, my sneaky habits became more evident. I tried quitting drugs on my own several times, but each period was short. I quit long enough to meet new people. Since I was a stay-at-home mom with three young ones and two school-age children, I ventured out and made friends with my children's friends' moms. One friend had three kids the same age as my older two children. Stephanie was beautiful. I nick-named her "Black Barbie." Her facial features were an exact copy of a Barbie doll, tall with long and silky dark brown hair, smooth chocolate-brown skin, perfectly shaped dark eyebrows, and clear, bright brown eyes. Stephanie and I found ourselves sneaking away to get high around our children's school schedules and our husbands' work hours. That lasted until her husband came home early one day and busted us. We both sat around talking about ways of staying clean together, but then I met two more women in the neighborhood who sold the drugs. Somehow, buying drugs from these women, in my mind, made getting high different.

I started hanging out with a group of women drug dealers. I should have learned my lesson from Detroit that there is no such thing as free drugs, but one young lady bought my story of being new in town from Detroit and decided to befriend me. She started pinching off her sack to give me kibbles and bits. Of course, I became one of her steady customers. Before I met her, I had shipped my youngest sister back to Detroit before moving out of the rinky-dink apartment. My sister made her way back to the new house to help me with my younger ones.

While my sister was my full-time sitter and I was still employable, I got a job at a bank in Glendale, California. Although that job was short-lived, I discovered the famous Glendale Mall while working there. It was well known around southern California that movie stars frequently shopped there. While walking through the mall, I spotted a small crowd of people circling Anne-Marie Johnson, who played Roger Thomas' girlfriend on the 1980s sitcom *What's Happening Now!* Another time, I was walking through the mall when I spotted this tall, slender guy walking toward me. He stood tall above the crowd. His face was so familiar, but I couldn't immediately place him. I stared at him from a long way off. Eventually, our eyes met. He started staring back at me. I'm sure I had no poker face. I felt my curious eyebrow expression. As we came closer, it hit me. It was Gregory Hines! My heart dropped to my feet. I didn't know how to react. I kept staring and so did he. When we were finally face to face, I shyly said, "Hi" and that was it. He spoke and smiled, and we both kept walking. I knew he knew I had figured out who he was, but I was over the moon with a frisson of excitement. I couldn't wait to get home to call my friends and tell them.

My new drug dealer friend knew about the celebrities who would visit the Glendale Mall since she'd lived in the area all her life. She seemed more impressed that I had a job and by my work dress attire. I didn't tell her, but I would take off from time to time with my little sister to go to Rodeo Drive to shop for clothes. We'd buy matching outfits and show up to places we were invited dressed like twins. This friend took a real liking to both my sister and me, and she started bringing drugs to my house. Once she saw my house, she was doubly impressed and started introducing me to her circle of friends. They happened to be the biggest drug dealers in the Pasadena/Altadena area. Little did I know I was again being pulled into the drug game like I had once been in Detroit. I'd often say to myself, "The game chose me. I didn't choose the game."

I got invitations to the drug dealers' private parties. They'd show off their large sums of cash and their fancy cars. One time, I was invited to the Rose Bowl Stadium with them. It was my first time there, and it was a big deal because I often talked about the 73rd Rose Bowl Game held on January 1, 1987 when the Arizona State Sun Devils defeated the Michigan Wolverines, and in 1988, how the Michigan State Spartans defeated the USC Trojans 20–17 in a bowl rematch. I didn't know what to expect, but when I got there, cars were lined up around the entire stadium. There were new cars, old cars, and classic cars; some were painted bright shiny colors; others were two-toned, and other cars changed colors as we passed by them. Some cars were rebuilt with hydraulics, bouncing up and down; some other cars moved in ways that hydraulics allowed. Then all the cars started up and took off, one at a time performing and showing off their car talent. We cruised the boulevards for hours. I'd never been cruising down the boulevard in Southern California or anywhere before, but now that I had, I thought it was the best time ever. I was hooked on my newfound crowd. Anybody who was somebody in the drug-selling business in Pasadena/Altadena area showed up, and since I knew very few somebodies, I felt like somebody hanging out with them. Not long after I experienced this "I have arrived" feeling, my downhill spiral began.

One day, I spotted a man walking up my driveway and appraising my house. My husband was working so his truck was not there to protect people from peeking in. Turns out, this man was out to sue my husband. I never found out exactly what had happened, but my husband ended up losing his truck-driving job. After that, his behavior became erratic. The overwhelming stress caused us to fight more. With five kids, no family to count on, and no real friends, I started using drugs more and became unable to manage any aspect of my life. We lost the house and went from one predicament to another, living with people we really didn't know with all our kids. Eventually, a young lady I had met at the community center when I first moved there helped us move into an apartment next door to her.

My drug use persisted to the point where everything fell apart at the seams. I didn't trust my husband's behavior anymore. I had become afraid of where his stress might lead him. Our fighting increased. I leaned on the girl who helped me get into the apartment for support. He had found another job, and I would take him to work. One day, I came out of our apartment to find our car was gone. I called and made a police report. Then one of my younger sons told me he had earlier seen his dad with the keys. When I questioned my neighbor, I was shocked to hear she had seen my car around the corner on another street. When my husband fell asleep, I walked to where she told me it was. In disbelief, I found it and drove it home. When I confronted my husband about why he had let me believe the car was stolen, he was silent. My concern for his mental health increased.

Later that night, I woke up choking from inhaling dense smoke. When I got up to inspect where the smoke was coming from, I discovered the kitchen cabinets were blazing. My husband had fallen asleep while cooking and a grease fire had started. I had to gather all my kids to get them out of the house. My neighbor friend called 911. That was the straw that broke the camel's back. I took off in the car with the kids and, fortunately, I got into a shelter for women and children that day.

I was still struggling with my addiction and sneaking around the shelter getting high. Then a lady, who was also in the shelter with her four kids, befriended me. She talked to me every day, and it didn't take her long to convince me we should get in my car and drive nearly six hours to another shelter, who knows where, with her four kids and my five kids. She made the phone call to ensure this shelter had room enough for both her family and mine. I got directions and off we went.

Lessons Learned

1. Defend, don't pretend.

2. Just because you don't have doesn't mean you can't get.

Questions for Reflection

getting francisco
around decided children little hall taught woman
trees home small told townspeople bought
mountain son met school house even three
thousands wild soon boy john took road know first huge
white pm people next learned turned good quite man
daughter two fire family ended driving local showed california
san life support winter girl built big drive creek
just time frog high away oldest idea sonora became living
city mom shelter one moved women stove
devon started acres kids back land place eventually
called drove area town's april mountainside
meeting town wood day roads knew
passed maria experience immediately

Have you ever experienced culture shock? How are you better for that experience?

Have you relied on the kindness of strangers? When?

When have you started over again?

Do you have a second community outside of your family?

____

____

____

____

Chapter 4

Sonora

We got there. It turned out to be a mobile home park shelter for woman and children only. It was on acres and acres of land with horses. This place is where I learned for the first time about frog jumps. Frog jumping is a competition that takes place in two side-by-side locations at the Calaveras County Fairground. Frog jumps were the town's excitement. They attracted people from all over to come and watch.

I lived in Angels Camp for a short period before one of the counselors at the shelter suggested I join one of the support groups held in the next town. It was recommended by the same counselor that I move a half hour down the road to a women and children's shelter in the next town, named Sonora.

The townspeople called the Sonora region God's country. The town's population at that time was about 2,000. It was so refreshing to see the mountains and drive up and down one-lane dirt roads. I was intrigued by the danger of driving on roads without guardrails. The beauty of the mountainside was captivating. They didn't have bus service, and only six blocks of sidewalks, which were mainly in the downtown area. Exploring the area was staggering for a city girl like me. The kids and I often drove up the mountain—6,000 feet—to Pine Crest Lake Resort. I was fascinated with the landscape—a beautiful sky-blue lake, in the middle of the mountains, surrounded by thousands and thousands of pine trees in various shades of green.

In the summer, the kids and I would drive up every day. We'd attend movies in the woods. We'd also drive through the woods, admiring the log cabins and wondering what it would be like to stay in one. The kids and I took our first hike in Strawberry, California, up a small mountain north of Pinecrest.

I focused on driving carefully up the mountain roads. In some places, the roads didn't have any barriers, so if you went too close to the edge, you could easily roll thousands of feet down the mountainside. The kids and I loved the awe-inspiring drive. I have since driven back to that place with a few of my grandkids. It seems important that the good memories of this place remain in my heart, and I share it with people I love with all my heart.

When my five kids and I moved to a shelter in downtown Sonora, two women from town, Maria and her partner, showed up to introduce themselves. They asked if I was interested in meeting advocates for my kids. The idea was for me to spend some time with myself. These two women were well known among the townspeople. They had been there for a while. They were assigned to take my oldest son. They asked if they could take him to play miniature golf. I figured that would be good for him. He was about nine at the time.

Maria, her partner, and I met at the local park. We talked a bit about my kids. I was convinced they were there to help. We decided they would come and take my oldest son off my hands regularly. But sometimes, these two would come and take my kids and me out to lunch. We would sit around talking. They would come over sometimes to hang out with the kids and play games.

They ended up not only taking my kids here and there during my shelter shuffle, but everywhere I moved; they kept in touch and even showed up unannounced sometimes. Even when I moved many miles away to the Bay Area, they showed up at my door. I said to myself, "These two women are taking advocacy quite seriously."

I eventually met and started dating the handsomest guy in town, Big John. The kids eased into getting to know him. We started doing lots of fun family things together.

I also met a man named Jim who was associated with the women's shelter. He became my landlord. He decided to rent me and my kids a two-bedroom apartment right down the road from the college.

I enrolled in the local community college in Columbia. Enrolling in college was my first attempt at getting my life on track. It seemed I had an entire town supporting me in ways I wouldn't fully understand until years later. I won a scholarship from the local gas company and was invited to a luncheon honoring me.

I joined my very first anonymous AA and NA Twelve-Step groups there. Life was looking up. I felt freedom I had never known before. I thought nothing of being a twenty-something African American woman showing up in a small, white town with five children. Everybody there knew who everybody else was, so the townspeople were quick to notice us. I know this because I drove down one road often and noticed them noticing me. Some people would talk to me at the local grocery store while others would stare from a distance.

One day, the kids and I were driving to the grocery store. Some guy, who seemed inebriated, was hitchhiking, and as we passed him, he yelled out, "Niggers!" I immediately got angry and plotted my revenge. I told the kids that on the way back when I blew the horn, they should all wave. As we passed him on the way back, I blew the horn, and we all waved—and he waved back. I watched his face turn beet red as he figured out who was cheerfully waving at him.

When I enrolled my kids in the elementary school, I had to have a meeting first with the school principal, a nurse, and the school counselor. The principal started out by saying the school had never had any "brown kids" attend before. I told them my oldest daughter had been in a gifted and talented program back in Pasadena. For whatever reason, in Sonora, she was labeled just very smart.

My youngest was in preschool. One day when I went to pick him up from school, one little girl blurted out, "Mom, look at that little brown boy." I felt the tension between the mom and the little girl as the mom tried to shush her. I chose not to add insult to injury by just keeping my eyes on my son, acting as if I hadn't heard anything.

I hung around the town's Alano Hall daily. I got to know quite a few people. The Alano Hall became a huge part of my social life. I attended dances, potlucks, and meetings there. People were kind and inclusive until one man at one meeting made a racist statement in reference to alcohol. He said, "We have a hard time getting that black ass monkey off our back."

Half the room turned and looked at me. I dared not flinch. I intuitively knew to ignore the statement and the stares because I couldn't afford to lose any support I had there.

As controversial as a white boy dating a black girl in a small white town was, Big John and I met in town regularly.

We thought very little of what everyone else was thinking or saying. Big John was new in recovery too. We met at a meeting. When we met, I had no idea it would turn into a twenty-year relationship. We ended up combining our families. He eventually brought his two kids from San Francisco, a boy and a girl, Li'l John and Celina. Although we had our separate places, most of the time our kids were together.

One of the women I met and became close friends with, Barbara, had called the hall looking for a ride. I immediately volunteered to pick her up. I drove two towns over to get her. She was moving back to town. We had never met before, but she was so wild and fun that I took to her right away. As I was driving her back to the hall, we got caught at a red light, and she just jumped out of the car and ran up the block. I immediately knew she was my kind of girl. I drove up the block and picked her up, and she said something that stuck with me forever: "I love my freedom."

Barbara introduced me to one of her friends, Janet. The three of us met up nearly every day at the Alano Club. We built such a tight bond that we decided to call ourselves the Ya-Ya Sisters. I celebrated fourteen months clean and sober with these two ladies and this mixed group of people, Native Americans, white folks, and me.

I told myself I fit right in. I learned how to sing Karaoke and line dance in cowboy bars and make dream catchers on the local reservation.

Many people from this mixed group, along with Barbara, took me from Sonora to Oakdale, Modesto, and Stockton for meetings. They taught me how to have real fun in recovery. They taught me the importance of being part of a group. And when I had my first experience with losing someone to an overdose, they taught me how to support the survivors.

They didn't know me from Adam, but they accepted me into their sober family. For a short while, and for the first time, I glimpsed what a strong sense of belonging was, and from then on, I could not forget or shake the feeling. Big John worked two-hours away in San Francisco while I stayed in Sonora with all the kids. One day, John did not come home. Two days later, he called to tell me he had relapsed. Soon after, I relapsed with him.

My relapse happened on a good day. Nothing had gone wrong. John was back on track. We were driving back to Sonora from his job in San Francisco. (He referred to San Francisco as "The City.") The weather changes there drastically in the summer months. It would be in the high nineties in Sonora, but in the low sixties in The City. Because of the temperature fluctuations, I ended up with a cold. Driving home from The City, I felt really bad, so we stopped at a drugstore. I got myself a bottle of Nyquil to ease the symptoms....

Before we reached home, I had drank the entire bottle.

I did not know it at the time, but the alcohol in the Nyquil had triggered my alcoholism. I was soon drinking heavily and back to smoking cocaine. Back then, the bad part about smoking cocaine in Sonora was the drive. My drug of choice was a one-hour and ten-minute drive away. Word spreads fast in a small town, so I soon found the town was talking about me.

One day, a man from town I did not know knocked on my door and told me he had a place for us. Where did that come from? The man owned lots of property around the town. He showed us the place. It was a four-bedroom house on two-and-a-half acres of land. We took the house.

We had regular visits on the property from wild rabbits, snakes, possums, skunks, deer, mountain lions, king snakes, small lizards, and field mice. We had a natural creek. Our neighbors all had alpacas, llamas, cows, chickens, roosters, and goats.

One day, the game warden visited, asking if we owned wild guinea hens. I was clueless. I had never heard of a guinea hen. I found out they were wild and had attacked the neighbor's roosters.

A creek down the hill behind our house and then curved around to the side, but when it rained a lot, the creek's banks would overflow, flooding our driveway. The house was built on a slope and sat 2,000 feet up in the foothills. The kids would find things they could float on and ride the creek to the end of our road.

Once in a while during winter, it would snow. Our source of heat was a wood burning stove. Knowing how to turn on the wall heater thermostat was the extent of my knowledge about how to heat a house, and this house had no thermostat. The kids and I had to figure out how to use the stove. The boys learned how to chop wood. The girls wore hoodies over their pajamas. I rushed out and bought us long underwear to help keep us warm. We took turns standing in front of the wood burner for hours at a time with the one extra-long barbecue fork we owned, twirling the wood for the fire to catch. It took my entire first winter to learn how to warm the place. The one time I got the wood burner hot, the roof nearly caught on fire. That's because I had decided lighter fluid was a good idea. The fire got going so strong and hot that I heard a roaring, rumbling sound. When I went outside to check the chimney, huge embers were flying out onto the roof. I stood there, stupefied, literally biting my fingernails. I was relieved when the fire died down and I didn't have to call the fire department. But another time, the fire department did have to come out and put in place the huge fans they use to get smoke out. The smoke was so thick that they left the fans there for a day. If my daughter April hadn't thrown flour on the stove fire I had started, I don't know where this story would have ended. Of course, a wood burning stove requires wood. I bought wood in town. However, when huge trees would fall in the neighborhood, I'd hear people outside during the day running their electric saws, cutting up the fallen trees for wood. When a couple of neighbors shared their wood with us, I learned I had been buying green wood. That was why my fires weren't burning. The townspeople who sold me wood knew I knew nothing about buying wood. By the next winter, I'd learned my lessons well.

Although winter was a hassle so we could stay warm, I basked in driving up the Sonora Pass on Highway 108, up the mountainside through the sugar pines and to Mi-Wuk Village with the kids to look out over the thousands of snow-topped pine trees covering a multitude of the hills, a true winter wonderland.

On one hand, I enjoyed the crisp clear beauty of my surroundings while living the mountainous life. On the other hand, I was in the throes of my "ism," living in this house. Soon my troubles began to spiral out of control in my newfound sanctuary. Using drugs took its toll again. My family split up in many different directions. Big John and I broke up. He took his kids with him to stay with his aunt in the Bay Area. My oldest son moved back to Detroit with his dad. I was left with my three younger children while my oldest daughter, April, moved out and got emancipated shortly after she turned sixteen. She ended up moving in with the two advocates I had now nicknamed AM and PM (Maria) based on their initials. They had built themselves a house out in the woods near a creek in Columbia. I was impressed because they built it from scratch with their own two hands. Only recently did I learn that they had been so busy being in the wilderness and under the moon and the stars that outdoors was their restroom. They took my daughter in and moved her into this two level, 400-square-foot wooden cabin. They eventually built an outhouse with showers under the moon and stars. April stayed with until she graduated from high school. They completely supported her while she worked at different restaurants for extra money. They even bought her her first car.

AM and PM proved they were serious about advocacy in a way I had not expected. On one of my occasional incarcerations—you will read about those in the next chapter—they dropped everything on their schedule and bought all three of my youngest kids tickets to Detroit. Maria got on a Greyhound and dropped them off at my mom's house at my request. Taking them to my mom's house was my last resort. It was my three younger kids' first experience living in Detroit for any long period.

I ended up getting out of jail, but I didn't do anything the judge ordered me to do while on probation. Cooperation was not my forte, so I ran away to the Bay Area. Sure enough, law enforcement came after me, brought me back to Sonora, and put me back in jail. AM and PM showed up—they were there for me again.

Eventually, AM and PM moved to Sebastopol, California. By the time my youngest son, Devon, turned fourteen, he had moved in with them. They got him through high school just like they had April. Devon was quite popular on his high school campus. I later learned he was the only brown boy in that high school. He had gotten a job at the local grocery store and did a commercial for them. I still have the ad he did, quite a historic moment for him in Sebastopol,

California. AM and PM and the townspeople had gotten Devon involved in the community. He learned to ride a unicycle and became the town's clown for festivals. He met lots of people—kids and their logging parents—who helped him learn a trade by living off the land. Devon taught himself symmetry art, which he still does today, and he turned it into a small business for himself. He told me art was healing for him. Devon's experience turned out wonderfully, except I missed watching him grow up, and he didn't have me, his mom. When he told me that at his graduation, I had a deep, painful, and overwhelming realization. I'd had no idea about the trauma I passed down to all of my children. A moment of clarity now set in, and I couldn't find an escape from the heartbreaking reality, not even one second of any kind of humor, which is what I normally used to cope, to process the trepidation of this reality.

After Devon's graduation ceremony, AM and I had a long talk. She disclosed that she had recently joined a Twelve-Step program. I immediately passed her my two-year coin and shared my experience with her. All those years when I was on drugs and alcohol, AM was there for my kids. At the end of the day, I was able to be there to support her on her journey of recovery.

This woman put absolutely no conditions on helping me with my kids, even though she and PM broke up when AM was drinking. For me, they were angels with skin. I have no idea why they invested their time, money, and emotions into my family. What I do know is they stopped going across the world to support people in Africa and started supporting my family instead. They shared my kids with me.

It's funny, though, how our relationship made a 360-degree circle. It's as if our cycle of life is complete now, and we're bonded for the rest of our lives. And it all started with support from complete strangers whom I have come to love dearly.

No one ever knows how life's circumstances can change. My California odyssey is a pretty bizarre and wild story, but I hope you found something in it that helped open your mind to fate. I am convinced fate brought me to Sonora to meet the people I would wind up making lifelong friendships with. Their support reminds me that you never know who will end up helping you. Keep an open mind.

Lessons Learned

1. Accept help even when you don't want to ask.

2. Just try. You might just succeed.

Questions for Reflection

Have you ever experienced discrimination? What did you learn from it?

____

____

____

____

When has it seemed like something in your life was the result of fate?

____

____

____

____

Do you have a support team or a particular person you can rely on no matter what?

____

____

____

____

How are you involved in your local community? How would you like to be involved?

____

____

____

____

Chapter 5

Three Times in Jail

Waking up three years in a row on my belly button on my birthday in the county jail was not among the best of my experiences. My first time being released from the county jail, Big John and I left through the lobby talking about why he had come to pick me up. He told me he had asked the jailers to bring him his woman. He told me I had actually been locked up for more than eight hours. That was significant because he and I had the same charges. The jail had fingerprinted him, but it let him go immediately. He expected the same would happen to me. He was home waiting for a phone call, but he was never called. He told me he got impatient, drove down to the jail, and told the officers he was there to pick me up.

That was my first experience with the local county jail. The judge had sentenced both John and me to one day in jail. The prosecutor did not agree with such leniency. During our court session, the prosecutor expressed frustration when the judge started our court appearance with a conversation about how my stepson and his friends had taken the high-school basketball team to the state finals that year. Little did I know we had often sat in the bleachers at the high school basketball games with the judge who would sentence us for stealing from the local grocery store. At that time, the local stores in Sonora had the honor system, meaning none of the stores had security guards. The entire town knew exactly who we were. We were the mixed-race couple who had combined our families. My five black kids and his two white kids, all living together in a small, predominantly white town, were bound to be closely observed. Before we had combined our families and moved in together, Big John had previously lived in an apartment across the street from one of the long-time local sheriffs. This man spied on us often.

I was signed up on a probation order. I would not comply with the very first sentence, which read “Obey all laws.” I didn’t even read it until a couple of jail visits later. My second jail visit, I came to—sort of like coming to from a blackout—surrounded by a bunch of white girls. All of them were familiar with each other. Given the town’s small population, everyone in the drug community hung around town with each other. I hadn’t made any drug friends in Sonora because my drug of choice was smoking cocaine, which was now called crack. The closest town where my drug of choice was available was Stockton. The drive took an hour one way—a long drive for a drug run. The women were each telling their stories about their meth labs. I had no clue what a meth lab was until one of the jailers pulled me out of my cell to describe the chemicals used to set up a lab. He explained it like it was everything under the kitchen sink. I had the audacity to turn my nose up at the idea, as if my drug of choice were somehow different. I have since learned we all disparagingly compare our drug choices to others’ drug choices in an effort not to feel bad about what we are doing. Isn’t that something?

My third jail visit, the sergeant kept me in the holding cell. He came in and slammed the door as hard as he could. He placed his foot on the hard cement bench like it was his footstool. When I looked up at him, he crossed-folded his arms. He stared me in the eye for one of the longest silent eye stares I have ever encountered. His words were spoken with deep anguish. "Every time you come to my jail, it never runs smoothly! What do you want us to do with you?" I calmly and sincerely replied, "Send me home." He turned away in utter disgust, damn-near shattering the plexiglass when he slammed the jail cell door.

One time, I was jailed with the daughter of one of the jail nurses. Her left eye was popped out of her head to two times the size of her other eye. The corner of her eye was filled with oozing puss, and her eye was bloodshot red and swollen from being burned in an explosion. She had been in a blown-up meth lab accident. Her mother, literally, was the one rolling around meds to every jail dorm.

I was at the center of many contentious moments, being the only black coming back and forth, year after year to this small-town, county jail. One of the jail's regular patrons came toward me, limping from side to side. One of her legs was shorter than the other. She brought another girl with her. She introduced herself as "Shot" and her friend as "Call." She began, "Whatever we say...." I interrupted her by saying, "I don't know you, Shot and Call, but whatever you shoot and call, you're both going to get out of my face." The entire dorm erupted in loud chatter. Another girl went over to my mattress and pushed it onto the floor. I started making a grand announcement, "If anybody else touches my stuff..." but before I could complete my sentence, the room erupted with screaming and a bunch of girls got in my face.

The building shook like a 6.0 earthquake as several jailers ran to the dorm to separate me from the general population.

The jailers decided I could not be housed in general population, and I was better off in a cell by myself until they figured out what to do. While in the general population, one of the jailers would open the dorm door and yell across the room, “Hey, brown girl, you.” I’d ignore him, but it was no secret whom he was speaking to. It was clear they didn’t have any place there for people like me. That same jailer would come take me out of my one-man jail cell and feed me ice-cream sandwiches while I listened to his criminal activity outside of work. He caught his wife cheating with his best friend, so he broke into the best friend’s house and trashed his place. Oh, the stories I heard, and better yet, I learned the jailers really do listen in on your phone calls. One day, I was talking on the phone to Jeanette, my best friend Margie’s mom. I was telling her my hair was breaking out. She suggested I put raw egg on my hair. Most people know when you are in jail you have no access to things you normally have at home, but not two minutes after I hung up from that phone conversation, an egg rolled under the jail cell door. Just like that!

Finally, I was placed with the red jumpsuit ladies. I had no idea what the difference between an orange and a red jumpsuit was, but clearly, it was time for me to learn. One woman happened to be the wife of the town’s probation officer—the same probation officer I was assigned to. She kept driving drunk down those mountainside roads—the ones with no guardrails. If you rolled your car, you would find yourself rolling down anywhere from 2,000 to 6,000 feet. It was her seventh DUI. She was going to prison. They were sending the probation officer’s wife to prison. She really wasn’t talkative, but I was trying to collect as much information from her as I could. Once I got out of jail that time, I met her husband. I wanted so badly to ask questions, but I was only in the position to answer them.

The other young woman wearing a red jumpsuit was in for murder. She talked, and I asked. She described the scene. Her story was pretty dark and gory. She had been on a meth run for twenty-plus days. She repeatedly spoke of the fingerprints being too high up the wall to be hers.

I heard stories about meth and heroine episodes. One story stood out. A woman came into the cell as if she were starving. She said, "I don't know how much weight I want to gain. I was just here ten days ago. I went to the house where they put me. I met up with some friends, and just before I was getting ready to take my second shot, the cops came and grabbed me. They saved me from myself." I thought, *She was saved from herself.* Her statement resonated with me. I felt I needed to be saved, but I had no one saving me. I was drowning in my own sea of sadness and despair about being in jail.

A judge granted me permission to get out of jail to attend April's graduation. I had asked for permission from the California Supreme Court judge during my sentencing. I later discovered the judge's sister was close friends with my kids' advocates, AM and PM. It's a small town after all. A day before the graduation, one of the jailers brought the dress to the dorm that Big John had dropped off for me to wear. The jailer showed it off, like it was a hot item for sale, to the other women in the dorm. He opened the dorm door with the dress hanging off his fingertip. Opening the door got everyone's attention, but the dress hanging off his pointer finger added a little curiosity.

The jailer proceeded to make an announcement—I had no idea what he was about to say. He said, "Winonna has some really nice friends. Her friend brought this dress for her to wear to her daughter's graduation." I was stunned because I instinctively knew this announcement would turn out to be trouble.

Trouble was an understatement. Although, none of the women were friendly toward me or even included me in any conversations or acknowledged my presence, suddenly everyone had a demand. One wanted me to bring back cigarettes. They were all pretty clear and graphic in telling me the process for getting things into the jail. I listened but said nothing. I had already made my mind up that I wasn't going to meet any of their demands.

On the other side of their demands were their heartbreaking stories. One woman came over to my bunk crying, telling me how hurt she was because her mom had died while she was in jail and she had been denied the privilege to attend the funeral. Another woman told me a story about how when her son had died, she also got the same denial. Pretty soon, the chatter got louder. It became clear that being let out to attend a graduation ceremony was not a privilege normally granted.

The day came for me to join my family, who had flown in from Detroit. I attended the graduation and went to dinner after the ceremony. I had been given a window of time from the judge and the jail to return. I returned casually, two hours past my deadline, elated. Once I got in the jail, that casual elated attitude was wiped off my face by the sergeant and another jailer who drilled me for hours about not adhering to the orders. I got two weeks added to my sentence.

My gratitude for the opportunity to go to the graduation was washed away by several issues. The first was I now had two weeks longer to be in this dorm with women who were doubly upset with me because I got to go to my daughter's high school graduation. And another issue was I hadn't obeyed the in-house rule to bring back cigarettes and other requested goodies.

The day I counted that the two extra weeks were up, I stood at the dorm window for hours like a child waiting to get off punishment. The jailers purposefully came to that dorm to get people out for different reasons. They intentionally ignored me and left without saying one word about when I would be let out. By the time they let me out that day, I had given up and resigned myself to the idea that they had no plans of keeping their word, much like I didn't keep my word and return on time. That was my hard lesson on keeping my word. Today, keeping my word helps me build integrity.

Lessons Learned

1. Some things have to happen more than once for you to learn.

2. Jail cells aren't Motel 6.

Questions for Reflection

black talking keeping
people pretty stores saved jumpsuit county sonora
telling probation phone really clear two word best
day small red sentence population court
knew friends combined
meth lab local judge call jail graduation
together brought wife couple cell first time shot
conversation friend woman door basketball
jailers attend let one john kids prosecutor side
white told weeks often announcement
girl face hours dress
story school left went idea hard
back dorm women eye high
stories bring going
little home go drug given
none know town jailer year choice just
waiting pick called big
asked general started entire across
families

Do you keep your word? When was a time you didn't? What lesson did you learn from it?

____

Have you ever had to miss a very important event?

____

Are you a victim or a hero in your life?

____

Do you have a Big John in your life?

____

____

____

____

Chapter 6

The Struggle Is Real

Being Challenged to Change

I continued to have difficulty staying clean. I could stop drinking and drugging, but I couldn't stop starting again. My struggle in connecting with people in different AA/NA groups became apparent. I joined a group in Oakland. I had a lot of fun with that group. I worked hard at recreating the same fun I had experienced in Sonora. Unfortunately, there was no recreation. I had fallen farther down the scale in my addiction.

I participated in talent shows with the group and got involved with doing service work. There was one young African American lady in the group I will never forget. She was about my age, early thirties. She witnessed my struggle and emotionally cornered me. She said, "Winonna, there's no reason why you are not doing exactly what I'm doing." She had a promising career working for Microsoft. She lived alone in her own apartment and had a new car. I longed for what she had.

I sat there silently thinking about what she had said. Her words touched a spot that spoke to my soul. It was pretty painful to hear that from someone I barely knew. It seemed as if she saw past my mask. I knew what she was talking about. I hadn't put very much effort into my recovery. I had spent years joining these groups and having fun, but I wasn't doing quite what it takes to secure and consolidate my recovery. I hung out with her for a while.

Before long, I got myself a spiritual advisor. This woman was the director of a Twelve-Step program in San Francisco. One day, she purchased a new car—a drop-top Mustang. She decided to take me on a road trip to San Diego on one of her business trips. She wanted to talk with me. She told me she understood I was a very capable and intelligent woman. She also told me I was a well-kept woman, meaning I had a man taking care of me while I didn't take any responsibility for myself. I did not understand what she meant at the time, but in hindsight I get it. As long as I was with Big John enabling my addiction, I didn't have to work or do anything for my recovery, I was just expecting something different to happen while doing the same thing. A part of me I had never connected with listened to her, and it stuck with me.

I also listened to other people in the Oakland group. The things they said bothered me. It bothered me because they were right. They were right that I hadn't been doing very much for myself as far as looking inward to find the reasons I continued to struggle. I had never looked at why I punished myself so extensively. I had never looked at why I drank and drugged from the beginning. It was easy not to think about it because it was a lot of very painful stuff to examine, and I couldn't connect the dots on much of it without help. It would be a very long time before I accepted help. I had to go through a lot more pain, anguish, and terrible situations.

A Moment of Resilience

Big John drove from the Bay Area, packed up my things, and moved my three younger children and me into his apartment there. We lived directly across the street from the El Cerrito Fire Department. Driving up and down the main road every night at 2 a.m. to go buy crack turned out to be a bad idea when your car and the police car were the only two cars on the road most nights. It didn't take long for the fire department and police department to collaborate and evict us. My special gift of finding shelters worked in our favor. Although Big John could have stayed with his aunt, he chose to stick close by.

We lived in different shelters for a while. I got clean enough to apply for a job. The job happened to be working for a shelter. At that job, I learned to make sure I not only tapped into my Twelve-Step program, but to take care of the wreckage I had caused in the past because if I didn't, that wreckage would catch up to me.

I was working diligently. I was very much a part of the community of homeless people, I was looking good and felt good too. I was even driving a Benz—to me, a sign of doing well. I dressed up every day in my blazers and panty hose.

I was hired to work with a caseload of 100 women. The shelter was set up in a building sort of like a warehouse open space, sectioned off. There were several offices, the kitchen, and the dining area; the men and women had separate sleeping quarters. My duties included intake of individuals entering the shelter, managing the dorm area's tidiness, administering people's meds, helping them schedule appointments, and helping them manage their personal needs with toiletries, and I doled out the toiletries. But what I did not do was the work required to sustain my recovery.

Also, I did not look back at or consider making amends for any of the wreckage I had left in El Cerrito, let alone any wreckage from Sonora.

At the shelter during my shift, a coworker asked me to drive her to the bus station, so I did. I left my post to drive my coworker to the bus. When we got there, I mistakenly turned the wrong way into the bus station right in front of a cop. The cop pulled me over. Not only did I get a ticket—I ended up going to jail because I had been driving without a driver's license.

I didn't get fired. In fact, when I called work the next day, they told me they wanted to put me on contract and have me work at a shelter in a more dangerous area. I would be working overnight by myself with forty-eight women and fifteen men. The blessing was, because I had the skills to work with the homeless and the drug community, I started assigning people whom I could trust to help me out in that shelter overnight. I worked that shelter overnight for two weeks with no incidents. My coworkers saw I was very capable of handling strenuous and dangerous, difficult situations, so I ended up getting a promotion.

Big John and I finally found permanent housing. Once we got the new place, Big John's aunt took us shopping and bought us brand new furniture for the entire place.

I quit my job and got loaded the next week. It was another relapse on all fronts. We ran out of money, and I started stealing to buy more crack. I got caught stealing in the Bay Area. The same behavior that I had kept going back to jail for in Sonora. Tsk, tsk.

You Can Run, But You Can't Hide

I decided to fight the shoplifting charge and take it to trial. When I got to trial, the police officer they put on the stand was not the one who had arrested me. The arresting officer and I had made arrangements about what we were and were not going to say. The judge had agreed to these terms, but the new cop didn't stick to the plan. This impostor cop claimed he was the one who had arrested me. The judge had ruled out some things that weren't supposed to be brought up, but this cop brought them up, and the judge did not throw out my case. Instead, he decided to start over and set another trial date. I felt like they were out to get me. I thought I was going to prison.

When Big John and I left that courtroom, he took me directly to the Greyhound bus station. He put me on a bus to Detroit. I went to Detroit believing it was the only thing I could do.

It was the beginning of a transition that would lead to my living with my grandparents and my dad, learning to live with my disease of addiction, and reaching the level I needed to reach before I cleaned up for good. The lesson I had to learn was that the thing I was running away from was actually the thing I had to run to.

I arrived in Detroit and surprised my grandparents by showing up at their house. "Hey, here I am." They hadn't expected me, but they let me in, and they were happy to see me. It had been some years since we had been together. My grandmother looked me up and down, head to toe, like always and decided I looked okay—I was still wearing the three-piece suit I'd worn to my trial. Honestly, I was so mixed up and unstable, but I was home.

For the first time after spending lots of time at my grandparents' house, I actually really paid attention to my dad and we spent some quality time together. Those were the good times. My grandmother set the table as she always did. She asked me what my favorite dish was. She added my favorite dish to everybody else's favorite dish for breakfast and dinner.

The rule was, we come to the table after we wash our face, wash our hands, and make up our bed. Grandma was in a wheelchair, handicapped from the stroke, but she cooked the meals. We were having family time, and even in my late thirties it was familiar to me from my childhood. It was refreshing; memories of how secure I felt at my grandparents' house as a child flooded my mind. Being there as an adult, having secretly run away from the law but spending time with my family, and totally not even thinking about the troubles that had put me in such a familiar place, made me feel loved again.

I took the opportunity to engulf myself in every second of it. I learned my grandparents' daily routine. Besides breakfast and dinner at the table together, they played a competitive game of dominoes against each other on Tuesdays and Thursdays at 7 p.m. Wednesdays they played cards, and on Sunday, my grandfather washed my grandmother's feet.

One most important factor remained. Here I was, an adult in the house with my grandparents and my dad. My dad had lived with his parents all my life, but he was always out of sight. Many times, visiting my grandparents' house when I was a child, I forgot he was there. For the first time, I realized the dynamics between my dad and me. Being at my grandparents' house when I was young was all about me going outside and playing. Now it was about my relationships with my family members.

Once I learned my grandparents' routine, I sneakily started smoking crack and blowing the smoke out the bedroom window. My dad was in his room, which was kitty-corner to mine. One day I heard an air freshener spraying outside my door. I snatched open the door to see my dad spraying. He said, "Are you in there smoking crack?" I responded in an emotionally charged whisper, "Why are you telling on me?" I knew my grandparents were downstairs listening to him spraying.

Seconds later, my grandmother yelled my dad's name and asked, "What's going on up there?" My dad said, "Nothing," and went back to his room. I rushed in after him, bursting in without knocking. I yelled at him. For some reason, he decided to hide his liquor bottle under his pillow. I rushed over to his pillow while he went to open the window and immediately found the bottle. I took a big swig.

There I was in this space with my dad for the first time in my life looking at myself—he was like a mirror image of me. As I calmed down, we started to talk. I kept sipping from his bottle until he took it back and hid it again. He kept trying to hide it, and I kept finding it. It became a game of hide-and-go seek, and the evening ended in painful belly laughter with him for the first time I could recall.

A similar incident occurred a week later when I thought he was telling on me. He said, "Baby, I don't want you to end up like me." I sarcastically replied, "Let me say something to you. If there is something about me that reminds you of you, I'm sorry." I stormed off, rushing down the stairs.

My grandfather happened to be sitting at the bottom the stairs at his desk. I was certain he had heard the entire conversation because when I got to the bottom of the stairs, he said in a calm, quiet voice, "Hey, hey." I looked at him because he was kind of quiet about it. Then he pointed to the corner and said, "There are some boxing gloves over there in the corner." I couldn't believe how funny my grandfather was. He made quite a few serious situation very funny. He had a stoic sense of humor about his life after all the things that he had gone through.

My stay with Grandma and Grandpa was a time and space where, for the first time, I experienced a strong sense of wholeness in connection with my family. My grandparents were my human shield from the problems I was running away from and the problems I brought into their house. From time to time, I would come out of my room at the same time my dad would come out of his; we'd meet, and it was like meeting myself in the hallway.

The image of meeting myself in the hallway became so significant and so meaningful. My dad and I were bonding. As I said, my mother got pregnant with me when she was sixteen, and my father took off to join the Navy. My mother was left alone and pregnant, and all her family could say was what a damn shame it was. Even after my dad returned home from the Navy, I never really bonded with him. Now that I was constantly meeting him—myself—in the hallway, I could no longer ignore what I had felt to my core all my life. The reality of being a product of my father set in as I ran from the law. It turns out I would spend the last two years of my father's life with him and my family, all of us getting to know each other. I learned a lot about who I was by looking at my reflection in my dad's defects.

Dad's Story, and How Not to Project onto Others

The first sixteen years of my life were spent with my mom and my stepdad. My dad had joined the Navy, then got out, got married, had my half-sister, become a heroin addict, and lived with my grandparents the rest of his life. His wife got shot and killed when my half-sister was seven.

My dad talked with me about what had happened when my mom got pregnant with me. He said he felt guilty. He said things like, “If I had stayed with your mom, things would have turned out different for you.”

I listened to his side of the story. I had never spent any real time with my dad. It turned out that running from the law was not the only real reason I went back to Detroit. It was to get to know my dad. Eventually, I would go back to California to face my troubles. It all turned out fine, by the way. Then, in 2004, my dad was hospitalized.

His sister called me to tell me my dad wanted badly to see me. I didn’t know that something serious was going on. I couldn’t imagine why my dad felt such a sense of urgency.

I flew back to Detroit. My aunt picked me up from the airport and drove me straight to the hospital. When I got to the hospital, the nurses said they had just taken him off the ventilator. He saw me and said, “Daughter, I want you to go in there and talk to the doctor, but I want you to listen more and say nothing.” I agreed but had no idea what this was all about.

I went off and talked to the doctor, who started by telling me my dad had cancer. It had started as skin cancer and then grown inside his body. He had fallen and broken his leg. They had to amputate it, and she told me they had taken the leg off because the cancer had eaten it up. She said the cancer was going to his brain. It was shocking information.

When I returned from speaking with the doctor, my dad had me come closer to him. He whispered that he wanted me to go to his friends, who all knew me from the day I was born, to get him some heroine. He told me he would die if he didn't get any. I was shocked and had to think about it for a long time.

After I finished talking to my dad, my aunt drove me straight to my grandparents' house. My Grandma had been in the waiting room at the hospital, waiting to see my dad. Because my dad requested that he and I and the doctor talk, no other family member was invited into the conversation. When my aunt pulled up in front of my grandparents' house, my grandparents pulled in right behind us.

My grandmother was upset. She seemed upset with me. I had no idea why until she said, "You took all the time talking to him." I didn't know what had happened, but my grandmother finally told me she wasn't able to talk with my dad because after I left, he had been placed back on the ventilator. Little did I know I had heard my dad's last words.

I felt bad for my grandmother. My dad was her son, whom she had been living with most of his life and who had been taking care of her, doing things she couldn't do because she'd been in a wheelchair ever since she'd had a stroke. She had counted on my dad. He would jump out of bed at the sound of her call and run errands to local stores to pick up items she needed right away, and now she didn't have him to count on. I wasn't there to help. I was living across the country. I flew back to California a few days later, feeling awful, mostly for my grandmother.

Nearly a week after I returned to California, the doctor phoned from the hospital. She wanted me sign papers to take my dad off life support. She presented me with convincing evidence that cancer had taken over his brain. My dad, the doctor, and I hadn't talked about any of this when I was in Detroit. The whole setup was that I was his oldest child, and my dad had called me over to acknowledge I was the oldest child. I did not connect or process any of this while I was there.

The final days of my dad's life became my responsibility. When the doctor called to tell me there was nothing more she could do, she eased me into the conversation by telling me a story about her grandfather's bout with cancer and what she had to face. I listened, but for me to pull the plug on my dad, have to fax papers to the hospital, and then sign papers to get his body from the hospital to the morgue—it was horrible!

Never Take Anyone for Granted

I was left making the decision to pull the plug on a man I barely knew. I was grateful I got to spend his last two years with him. That hit me pretty hard. Here I was thinking the whole time, *My grandmother is angry with me because she didn't get to hear his last words, and now I have to make this hard decision.*

I flew back to Detroit to wrap up loose ends for my dad and get it all done. I turned the funeral arrangements over to my family. I had been clean and sober for a little bit, but I went right back to doing what I always did. I didn't even make it to my father's funeral. That didn't turn out well. I looked bad in front of my family and friends. His friends decided to give me a bunch of drugs for free. Nothing's free. I was too busy doing them to go to the funeral. I really didn't want to go. I was already feeling bad that I'd had to make the decision to end his life.

I had spent very little time with my dad during his life. I had ripped and run the streets in Detroit, gone to California, and now come back to Detroit. I spent his last two years with him while I was running from the law. I didn't know my dad as well as I'd like to have known him, but I looked in the mirror after not showing up for his funeral and discovered I did know him. I couldn't separate my grief—I didn't know if I grieved his loss or my inability to show up with my family in a respectable way.

This all happened two years before my grandmother passed away in 2006.

It took me a total of four years before I got tired and decided to go to treatment. After I flew back to California, I lived in misery for two years before I got the call to come back to Detroit for my grandmother. Once my grandmother died, feeling pathetic and completely consumed with grief, I walked the streets of Detroit for nearly a year and a half.

Finally, I put myself in a treatment center in Memphis, Michigan. I didn't tell my family exactly where I was. I don't know why. I just called and said I was in Memphis, so they automatically thought it was Memphis, Tennessee, and I didn't correct them.

I was feeling better by going to counseling and treatment, but then my uncle, Sonny, weirdly and oddly a few weeks later, showed up at the very same facility. My uncle and I had both started smoking crack at the same time with the same people.

Uncle Sonny said, "We've been looking for you. Did you know I drove up and down the streets asking about your whereabouts? We thought you were dead!" I thought nothing of it and callously thought to myself, *Well, now he knows where I am.*

Two days later, I left the center, but before I left, I went to the counselor. She talked to me about the need for me to complete the program. I said, "Oh, I'm fine," and promptly left. I don't even remember how I had got ahold of any money, but I did, and within hours after leaving the program, I was at an abandoned house with the some of the same people I had been drinking and smoking crack with before. I wasn't getting high, but I kept trying. Crack had stopped working for me. I was clearly acting weird, but not the normal crack-smoking weird. I don't know exactly what I was behaving like, but everyone around me kept asking me if I was okay. And I said, "No, I'm not okay."

I immediately called my forever best friend, Margie. She said, "Bitch, I'm coming to get you before you kill yourself." At 5 a.m., she picked me up and drove me to the Detroit airport.

Instead of returning to California, at the last second, I called and begged Big John to help me change my ticket to Seattle. My oldest daughter, April, had been living in Seattle for quite a few years.

April picked me up from the airport, but she bluntly told me she'd had enough of my shenanigans. She took me straight to an AA meeting hall, which was two blocks from her place. I was surprised she knew where the meetings were. However, when we entered the meeting hall, no meetings were taking place.

A man was sitting near the food counter. Nobody else was in the entire building, so I asked him where the meetings were held. Pointing down the road, he said the meetings were a few streets over in the Green Building.

April drove me to the Green Building and handed me five dollars. As I was exiting the car, she said, "Don't come home until this meeting is over." She accelerated as soon as both of my feet were on the ground. The car door closed with the wind as she sped off.

I thought, *Geez, that was intense.*

I walked into the meeting and sat down with a group of strangers. They told me later that they had seen me holding onto my chair so tightly that my knuckles had turned white. I literally white-knuckled it through that meeting. They said they didn't know whether I was going to stay or bolt.

During the meeting, someone said if anyone had been sober thirty days or less, they should speak up and say their name so they could be welcomed. I had not felt welcomed the last days I was walking the streets of Detroit. One time I had gone to one of the most infamous crack houses in the neighborhood and they wouldn't let me in. I ruined everyone else's high. Now, something prompted me to speak up and introduce myself.

For the rest of the meeting, people went out of their way to personally welcome me, and they asked me to come back the next day.

That's how my recovery began.

I've been with that group of people for fourteen years now.

Lessons Learned

1. Resilience begins in real silence.
2. If you are going to run, run to family.

Questions for Reflection

building away something
wreckage
streets looked meeting cop know
job place
family two drove shelter
child always go bad people life lived
wanted back detroit area set road
working one big trial grandmother work dad's say nothing
hospital group time even told doctor thing living
asked car put kept days decided aunt listened
later let right
running run happened thought dad lot cancer first smoking
good last help new spent years john program telling
law day left went house learned
different took things felt started called recovery
room grandparents long california knew bus
going turned crack talk looking
want became

Have you ever felt distance between you and a family member, only to realize you had something in common? What did you learn from that experience?

Have you ever felt sick of yourself? What did you do to get well?

Have you been able to create a relationship with a family member you hardly know? How is your relationship today?

____

____

____

____

____

What was your lesson that had to be repeated and repeated until learned?

____

____

____

____

____

Chapter 7

Life in Recovery

Be Ready to Be Positively Influenced

My recovery celebration date is October 12. That date is an important one to me because my dearest grandmother's birthday is the day before.

My grandma, whom I adored so much, was significant to my recovery. I know people think about angels and all that stuff, but I feel like my recovery is pretty much honoring her. She didn't get a chance to see me clean and sober, but I know she prayed for me every day when she was alive. It was her way. Her message was clear. To this day, I'm unable to shake her last stare down before she passed.

Over the course of fourteen years in recovery, a lot of reality happens. Of course, I have another story to tell you. Earlier, I talked about facing my father, who mirrored who I am. I was told by my mom I was just like my dad when I was younger, but I didn't believe it, nor did I know what she meant.

When I looked in the mirror before, I didn't see anything. But now that I'm sober, I look in the mirror and see my authentic self. I decided long ago that my mother and father would define who I am. I can see how far I've come from my days of running around to living with intent and purpose. How I got here wasn't easy.

I continue reciting positive affirmations every day—because, really, fourteen years of sobriety is a very short period. I've accomplished a lot compared to where I was, but those accomplishments are short lived.

I've come to learn I'm driven. I am driven to prove I do not fit into the checked boxes society has tried to place me in. I am driven to prove that my black skin will not determine my destination. I am driven to prove I am someone, even if I don't have all the material possessions society tells me I need. I am driven not to die a practicing drug addict and drunk. I am driven to believe I was born with a crown that the people who raised me could not see. I am driven to believe that the people who influenced me saw something in me; although uncertain of what it was, they felt compelled to help me. As I stay clean and sober, my crown straightens out and my queenship appears more apparent. I am! Therefore, I set out to walk the path laid before me.

My number-one concern is how I can be of service to God and helpful to someone else. Working in human services, being a certified recovery coach, I work with people one-on-one, and I ask them questions to try to find what drives them and what their goals are. I feel like I'm holding their hands, working side by side with them, and being a good listener. I become their number-one cheerleader. Their positive results motivate me to do even more.

Recreate Yourself and Co-Create with God

I was six months sober when my recovery group encouraged me to go to school. In 2008, I enrolled in Everett Community College as a non-traditional student. I was afraid, but I went anyway. I was still foggy, but I got through in three years and graduated with my AA degree in 2011. When I graduated, it was with the most support I had ever had in my entire life. Not only did my classmates gravitate toward me and support me, but many of the people in my AA home group watched me like a hawk. People were befriending me from all around our area. They watched me like a hawk and took time to get to know me.

Tom, a guy in my homegroup who supported me, I call my brother. At one of my AA meetings, Tom called me to his table. He said, "I got a deal you can't refuse. I got a car for you. You can come and pick it up when you're ready." I had a blank stare. I wasn't quite sure I had heard what I had heard. I shook my head, but silently, and left to sit at another table to listen through the meeting. Once the meeting was over, I walked over to Tom's table to revisit what I had thought I had heard. When I questioned him, he replied, "Yeah, I got a car for ya, and you can come and pick it up whenever you're ready. But there is one condition. The condition is that you read the books and do the homework." I agreed and picked up the car that afternoon. I didn't know it at the time, but he was one of the people in the audience at my graduation. I found out he was there because the day after, I showed up at the meeting and he came over to me with a framed picture of me being handed my diploma. Flabbergasted, I cried. Other people from my AA meetings also came to the ceremony; they found me after to give me flowers and congratulate me. My oldest daughter, April, and my daughter Shay also showed up. What a difference support made! One of my first real goals had now been accomplished, and it motivated me to keep my word, meaning doing what I say I am going to do when I say I am going to do it, a lesson in integrity. I felt like God had given me a second chance at a first-class life.

Take Risks

A few days after I had settled into post-graduation, the group encouraged me to go on to the next level. I was afraid to move forward, but one of the people in my recovery group is an art teacher at the college. She pulled me aside and said, "Seattle Pacific University would love to have somebody like you." However, everyone seemed to be going to Western Washington, so I applied there. They denied me. Fortunately, I also applied to Seattle Pacific University and was accepted. It felt like that was where I was supposed to go.

I knew nothing about Seattle. One woman, Cheryl, who was a huge part of my recovery until the day she died, made a date with me. She got me in her car and drove me down the back roads to SPU. In my early days of sobriety, she would make a date with me, get me in her car, and drive me around the community to different AA meetings. I'd get in her car, she'd lock the doors, drive really slow, and start sharing her personal journey of what had led her to AA. Much of her story left me in a state of shock. I thought, *This white lady and her drinking story isn't much different from my drinking stories.* She shared convincing evidence of alcoholism, and I was floored. Eventually, she literally drove me all around Western Washington, introducing me to people in the meetings. When I was sensitive about something she's say, I thought, *Put on your big girl panties*. I hadn't divulged to her that I was afraid to drive from Everett to Seattle and that I was afraid of growing to the next level. I didn't have to. She knew, and she didn't tell me she was volunteering to show me a route to the school, As we passed by the school, she pointed out a half dozen places where meetings were held that we hadn't made it to yet. Before I understood what she was doing, I was wondering, *Why is she doing this?* Then it dawned on me. *She is showing me how to put on my big girl panties. I'm good.*

No, I wasn't. I was scared during my thirty-mile drive to school. Although not feeling it, I daily practiced positive affirmations in the mirror. When I shared my fear with my home group, I got an overwhelming response: "Oh yeah, of course you are afraid, and that's okay. You can be afraid, but you're going to do it anyway." And I did. I went every day, scared shitless, until the fear subsided. It's a good thing Cheryl had driven me there two weeks before school started and pointed out where the meetings were. A few of those meeting places became my regular pit stops before and after school. Thank goodness she had introduced me to some of the people she knew. Cheryl was more than thirty years sober, and she knew tons of people in the AA community. Turns out, I needed Cheryl. She was one old timer who remained a pillar in my recovery until she died. Actually, I had three pillars from the start of my recovery until they went to the big AA meeting in the sky—Cheryl, Betty, and Lizzette will be forever in my heart.

My forever best friend in recovery, Amy, drove me to the SPU campus to give me a confidence boost. She's a schoolteacher for God's sake—she got her degree years ago. When she got on campus, she had someone take a picture of us. She placed her arms around my shoulders and said, "When you graduate, we're going to have a party, and all your friends are going to be there." Not only did she plant a seed, but she produced a carrot—all my friends would be there.

Okay, but I was still scared.

You Are Who You Say You Are

I'm a non-traditional student, and I hang around lots of young people, but two young women specifically clung to me. One, Catherine, came from New York, and the other, Becka, was from Lynnwood. I don't know why we clung to each other, but we were like glue. It was the three of us all the way. These young women were the same age as my kids.

We made it through SPU together. I went to every class. I read the books and did the homework right alongside the two of them. For my birthday, a month before graduation, both Catherine and Becka took me to lunch at Paseo's, a Cuban sandwich place. Although it was a popular place, it was my first time there. After lunch, Becka placed her arm around me and said, "I want to tell you why you are important to me." Both she and Catherine recited the things important to them. Thunderstruck, tears welled up in my eyes. I couldn't stop the waterfall. I couldn't speak. But I thought there was no way I could have made it through my undergrad without the two of them.

The three of us took the same classes as much as we could. At one point, Becka took me to meet her parents. They had graduated from Seattle Pacific University, and so had her brother and sister. And here she was, taking me home to meet her parents who were my age.

Say Yes, Unless No Is Warranted

Out of nowhere, Becka's mom decided she was going to help me get my last seven credits to complete my degree.

She said, "I'm going to help you with your credits. As a matter of fact, when you graduate, I'm going to throw your graduation party." I said, "Wait a minute. You have to talk to my friend Amy because she told me in my first year at the university that she was going to throw me a party."

Becka's mom and Amy got together and planned the party. Let me tell about that party. I was blown away. Why? My best friend Margie and my friend Esther from Detroit both showed up.

On a phone call one day, I said to Margie, "You know, I'm about to graduate from the university." She said, "What? You're graduating? If you graduate, I'm coming."

Margie and I had phoned each other regularly. She knew about my life change. Before moving to Washington and making changes, my modus operandi was well known. I was the lowest of the low. My face was always on the bottom of someone else's shoe. People gossiped about me often. I had no dignity left in Detroit.

I opened a Facebook account and became friends there with many of my family members and friends. They have watched my journey via my Facebook posts. But nothing sealed the deal in terms of the acknowledgment and support of my changes like my two high school friends flying to Washington to witness my transformation and attend my graduation.

In many respects, the event unfolded unbelievably! Seriously, I reflected on the day Amy brought me to the university, sat me on a bench, put her arm around my neck, and told me she would throw me a party with all my friends there. It was a dream come true.

What Accomplishment Feels Like

Many of my recovery friends, my two closest long-time high school friends, and all my kids gathered for my party.

At graduation, one of my professors, who had made me retake her class because she did not accept the grade I earned the first time and challenged me, jumped up and hugged me as I walked off stage after getting my diploma. I didn't even like her that much. She probably didn't like me that much either. Of course, I was upset because she made me take the class twice. But she gave me a huge hug. That moment was captured by the *Seattle Times* photographer, and it made the front page the next day.

Forbes

Forbes is one of the old timers in my life. Let me tell you about my first Twelve-Step meeting in Everett where I met Forbes. This is what happened in his words:

> I was sitting in my usual spot—I always got there early, so I'd have my usual spot because it was next to the window. It has a view of the bay, so I always sat there. It's my favorite spot.
>
> People started showing up, and there was an empty seat next to me. Just before the meeting started, this woman walked in. She was a black woman I had never seen before. She came in and sat down in that empty seat. People get called on in the meeting, and they share. The woman sitting next to me got called on. She said her name was Winonna and it was her first meeting. She said her kids had dropped her off in front of the meeting hall and told her to go to a meeting and not to come back around them until she

had. She told us her story about being in Detroit and all the things she had done while she was there. It seemed that she was banned from Detroit, and so she went clear across the country to Seattle—and then she got banned from Seattle because of her behavior.

Well, her behavior was unacceptable, thank you very much. And she was drinking and using, and so she went north to Everett, and her behavior in Everett was so unacceptable that her kids told her that she had to get out of the house and go to AA. I mean, the things she'd done were just horrible and rancid. And she was drinking and drugging, and going with men she had known before, which was unacceptable, doing things with them that were unacceptable. She went on and on, and it was embarrassing, the things she had been doing while she was out there by herself drinking and drugging. I mean, I was embarrassed for her. I couldn't believe some of the things she said she had done, and so, she finally got done talking and telling us this was her first meeting and everything, and I couldn't believe it.

So, then they called on me. I said, "My name is Forbes and I'm an alcoholic." I said, "I just want to know one thing. I just have one question. Where was Winonna when I was drinking?"

Yeah, and everybody cracked up.

I think Winonna might have felt better after that. I hope she did. Anyway, she kept coming back. I'm glad she came to that meeting.

When I was in the community college, Forbes watched me closely. When we first met, he was stoic. I've since learned that he is one of the funniest people I know. One woman came up to me after one of our meetings and said, “I don’t know what you did to Forbes, but we’ve never seen him smile as much as we have since you’ve been here.” I would enter into the hall and walk straight over to the table where he sat, wave my hands to clear out anyone who was sitting next to him, and pull up a seat right next to him. He would pick up the wooden stick coffee stirrers and set them in the middle of the table, making barriers between him and me. One of the first lessons he taught me was about racism. He often recited his college chant, “Two, four, six, eight, we ain’t gonna integrate.” He felt compelled to share his personal experience with racism, and I felt compelled to listen. Here is the story he told me:

> This pre-Watts riot incident happened in 1962 when I was living and working in Los Angeles. My job involved driving to various locations in Los Angeles, and I learned that there were areas where certain racial gatherings were located. For instance, you had Beverly Hills; that was all white, and Hollywood was all white, and East LA was Mexicans, and Southern Los Angeles, Watts down that area, it was all black down there. And one day I had to go down to Southern Los Angeles. I was trying to locate somebody. So, I parked my car next to the curb, and I got out. It was kind of a business district, but there wasn’t anybody around. There wasn’t anybody on the street or anything, and I got the creepiest feeling that people were watching me, and it was hostile. It was unfriendly. I didn’t see anybody. It was just something that I felt, in the air, yeah. Like a feeling. I was walking around a little bit. I didn’t walk too far away from my car.
>
> This was two years before the Watts riot where they had that terrific riot where, you know, you didn’t

want to be a white person because if you were, you were going to get hurt because they were attacking white people when that riot first started. Because everything just was upside down. Even the cops got out of there. They gathered at first, but they left. They got out of there because everything was going crazy. And they were breaking into buildings, breaking into businesses, and stealing stuff and all that stuff. They were looting. And the Korean store owners were coming out with pistols and shooting at them, and yeah, everything was just upside down.

I turned around, got my car, and left. Yeah, it was that simple. And this was two years before the Watts thing, and before when I went down there, it was kind of like, you know, it wasn't like that. There was tension in the air, yeah. There was tension in the air.

What happened? There was an incident with the police. The police had pulled somebody over and people started gathering, and they were protesting the stop, and there was this big gathering of people, and the cops turned around and said, "Oh, oh, we're getting out of here," and they left. And then white people were starting to drive by in their cars—they just happened to be there—and they were being attacked in their cars. And bricks were being thrown, and it just got out of control. And if you were a white person, you tried to get out of there, and cars were being deliberately driven into other cars, and people were being pulled out of their cars when they were stopped and being attacked and being injured, and people were getting killed, and it just got way out of hand. And it went on, and then the fire started, and it went on for days. It was *the* riot. It was the first one.

That was the first riot I had ever experienced or knew of because I had been in that area two years before and had felt the hostile feeling. I was uncomfortable because I knew I was the only white guy in that neighborhood.

I had gone back to school because I was unemployed and unemployable. In 1965 and 1966, I lived in Bellingham. I got a student loan, went back to school in Billingham where the college was, and they had a concert. The guy's name was Witherspoon—Jimmy Witherspoon, was that his name? He was an entertainer, a singer. I didn't go to the concert. I was just sitting in a bar, and the guys from the concert, the singer, Jimmy Witherspoon, walked into the bar, and he sat down next to me. We started talking, and I told him, "You know, I used to live down there in Los Angeles," and he said that he was the first black person to move into Inglewood, which was a little north of Watts, and he was moving into the white area. And I saw something in the paper the other day that said Inglewood was all black neighborhoods now. Meeting Jimmy Witherspoon was nice. He's a cool guy.

There's a correlation between racism and the evolution of black people in sports in this country. Back in the day in the South, there was a saying that people used to keep blacks in their place. They had to be kept in their place, and there was a reason for that. I'm going to show you what the reason was here. I got these yearbooks. These were called the *Tyee*. They were put out every year by the University of Washington students, and we have a section on sports here. This is the basketball season for 1954. As we look in here, we see all these pictures, and you'll notice the color of the players—all these players are white. They're tall and they're lanky, but they're all white. See, page after page, both the Huskies and their opponents are all white for the 1954 season.

And then there's a picture of the JVs, the junior varsity. They're all white, and we go out here to the frosh, and this was the freshman class, and they're all…whoops…they're all white except for one player in the front row. He's black—the first black player on the basketball team at the University of Washington.

That would be 1954, winter quarter. Let's take a look at the following year. This is a 1955 yearbook, basketball 1955. Again, all white people. This is the varsity, pictures of the varsity basketball games, and all the Husky players are white. All the opponents are white, and then we go back to the JVs; they're all white. And the frosh, the freshman, there's a black player in the freshman team. Oh, yes, there is. Look at you, you spotted a black player on the JVs. That must be the one who was on the frosh team the last year; he's been promoted.

I've also got the 1955. I've got the 1956. This player was on the varsity in 1956. Now then, how does this relate to what's going on today? I've got some pictures from *The Seattle Times* from just this last week, and I'll show those to you. I got this picture here. What do you see there? You see all black people there at the basketball game, and this is December 2020.

The Huskies, they are all black. There's another one the same week, and what do we got here?

So, how is this relating? How this relates to what was going on with the saying that they had up in the South back in the day about black people. "Give them an inch and they'll take a mile." That was the saying in the South back in the day. Now, what day was that?

That would have been 1954 or 1953 back in the day. Before 1954, they say, "Give them an inch, they'll take a mile." And this picture of all blacks proves it, right? One black guy got on the JV team. He got on the frosh to start with and went from frosh to JV. The same black guy went to varsity after that. They took the inch, and now in 2020, the mile. See what happened? This was the belief among white people in my generation. People say, "Well, yeah, that's because they're better athletes," but the rebuttal to that is, "Well, yeah, but they cheat." They jump higher and they run faster.

When I went to the University of Washington, protests were happening everywhere.

It's just that's the way it was. I went there in the fall of 1953. And I remember a sociology class—the instructor was saying that there was some odd values or thoughts or morals, I guess you'd call them, that people have in different areas. Like at the University of Washington, which was the rainiest campus in the United States; nobody had an umbrella on the rainiest campus in United States. Nobody had an umbrella. You just didn't take an umbrella. You just didn't do that. It's a way of life here in Washington State. It was unacceptable; you just didn't do it. And I remember being in a football game at the Husky Stadium on a rainy day when I was a freshman and this couple showed up there. A black couple, man and woman, in the student section—they showed up and came in and sat down and pulled out an umbrella. And they

> were sitting there under this umbrella and people were reacting to that, not only because they had an umbrella, but I suppose because they were black as well. They were throwing apple cores at them and throwing junk at them and stuff because you just didn't do that. They brought attention to themselves by just coming to a game; they were black, but they added another layer by bringing an umbrella. The unacceptability. The guy got mad, but they just didn't get what was happening. And besides being black, they were the only black people in the crowd.

It was more than a notion for Forbes to share his relatable experiences with me. Forbes, as an older white male who had lived through the crucial period of the 1950s and '60s, felt compelled to share his personal experiences with me, a black woman in recovery in a dominantly white recovery community. Not everybody makes it to recovery.

RIP David

One of the most difficult things I've learned to live with in recovery is that not everyone makes it.

I'm recalling an example from about six years ago. My bunion hurt because I had to wear fancy boots to the life celebration. My stomach hurt because my friend David had died from an alcoholic seizure in his sleep. It makes me sick. My heart hurt because the pain of losing my friend was stuck there. And my head hurt because the memories we made were flooding my brain. My soul hurt because David was a schoolteacher for more than twenty years. His students loved him, their parents loved him, and he was loved by his entire school district, but no one knew what was happening to him. I knew. I knew because he told me his story. But what he didn't do is believe that he was an alcoholic. Funny how he kept calling me over and we kept coming around to the subject. His story is much like the story where the man stopped drinking, worked until he retired, pulled out his slippers, sat on his recliner, and drank himself to death in a very short time.

David stopped drinking in college because of the hangovers and a few other consequences, but he thought nothing of picking up a drink twenty-five years later—not drinking every day, just here and there. David would never identify himself as an alcoholic because he had finished college and gotten the job he loved. He made his career. It was all good.

When the first seizure happened, David bit his tongue in his sleep and needed stitches. He was puzzled, but he put it off. The next seizure happened in his Jeep on his way to work. He rolled the Jeep, broke his ribs, and had to wear a back brace. He couldn't work for many weeks. But David still wouldn't hear that perhaps alcohol may have caused his problem. He kept calling me to hang out, and he would talk about my dull social life in the Twelve-Step program.

He didn't want to hear about his drinking because drinking made him social. We went out dancing and to the movies, had homemade lunches and dinners together, and dear, he was just such a fun guy all around.

Being a kindergarten and first grade teacher, he had to be a blast, right? Amy, my forever best friend in recovery, introduced us. They worked together for years. The school did a wonderful job on his memorial. There must have been thousands of notes from students, parents, and his colleagues. All those years of teaching, he brought joy to so many parents and students who had him when they were young.

Well, I spoke to his sister and brother-in-law at the memorial. They told me they found paperwork he ignored from the doctors who wanted to run further tests because they were curious why a man would suddenly start to have seizures at age fifty-two.

David's life was teaching; he did it well. He will be missed, but Lord, my soul aches knowing what I know. I couldn't tell a soul at that memorial. No, no. Although social creatures, those following the straight and narrow would never believe it. The longer I live this way of life and the more I see, the more I learn. Rest in peace, David.

Lessons Learned

1. Do what excites you.
2. Be true to yourself first.

Questions for Reflection

table although coming
compelled took
umbrella started
class happened cheryl
place white recovery
look
player afraid went left story sat cars felt basketball
frosh put believe one around party riot kept
something everett los
parents college back school group date
just going
people knew seattle
told
made two life things pulled
stuff unacceptable
angeles guy black drinking woman next
time friends sitting
driven picture tell say course
sober first day
every
days meeting know
student
thought go years aa called
washington hurt even
amy drive car university yeah
david community
three meetings forbes friend varsity
someone showed good last graduation

How have stories from people of a different race, religion, or background helped you better understand their perspective?

Do you know someone whose bad decisions ended in their death? What did you learn from that experience?

How have you achieved? Where have you soared?

When did you start over again into a chapter of your life that you can see was soulfully yours?

____

____

____

____

Chapter 8

Caretaking

I completed my seven credits over the summer of 2014 and received my degree in communications, journalism tract, in the mail a couple of days before Christmas. I struggled throughout my university experience. My overall grades were average, but of course, I wished for excellence. My last two classes were a hint of where I might be headed next, although it's taken years to figure out. Both classes, "Family Communication" and "Troubled Families," were easy. Taking these classes was the first time I got all A's in one quarter. It was an exciting, revealing moment.

I started doing what graduates do—searching for work. I had made myself a promise to work on self-presentation. I had extensive dental work done so I would have a presentable smile. Drugs had destroyed my teeth, causing them to crumble from decay.

It took six months of searching to find a good fitting job. I got hired at a recovery center for women and children. On my first day at work, as I settled in, I got a call telling me my daughter Shay had been in an accident—I could never have imagined how that call would change my life.

I waited around to hear from my oldest daughter, April. She had taken Shay to the hospital but took her home after. I got a text from Shay a few days later that said, "I need help." She attached MapQuest directions to her location. I picked her up at her apartment where she had been left alone.

Shay couldn't talk. I took her to the hospital where the doctor accused her of being on drugs. Her pupils were pinned, which is viewed as a sign of opioid use. I spoke up clearly and said, "No, sir. This is not a case of drug use, and I cannot take her home in this condition. I'm not taking her home because I know."

I requested a hospital social worker. After I told the social worker everything, they decided to send Shay to the psych ward. I got a call from the psych ward the next day. They told me to come get her. I got Shay and took her back to the emergency department, and finally, a doctor ordered an MRI.

On July 1, 2015, I posted the following on Facebook:

> My baby has an abnormal MRI—that's why she can't talk. Finally, a doctor heard me, went beyond this hospital emergency policy crap, and looked further. I'm pissed to high heaven at the treatment my daughter got from a couple of doctors saying it was mental so they sent her to Compass Health's psychiatric ward. I knew something was wrong and begged the doctor, even argued with him, and refused to take my child home in this condition. All said and done, she is being admitted tonight. I am grateful to finally be headed toward the proper treatment for her.

The MRI showed that Shay had massive lesions. Her brain had attacked itself, leaving the lesions. We were able to trace the cause of the accident. The receptors that wake you up and put you to sleep were severed by the lesions, causing Shay to fall asleep while driving at the wheel. Falling asleep then caused her to crash into the back of a car that was sitting at a red light. The police report stated that Shay's airbag had deployed and there were possible injuries, but Shay had refused assistance and they took her home. The brain lesions left permanent brain damage, and on top of that, the air bag caused Traumatic Brain Injury. Shay had two children she needed help with. I quit my job and jumped in with both feet to help her. I was up for the challenge of assisting her with her health, wellbeing, and her kids. It became my sole purpose. I put my best foot forward. As a result, Shay has not missed one doctor's appointment in six years and counting.

Frustrated with the politics of the medical system and the beast of insurance companies and ridiculous three-month waits for referral approvals, I got angry and told the doctor I was taking Shay to the Mayo Clinic. Her doctor drew in closer to me and nearly whispered. The question she posed changed everything: "How will you get her on the plane?" Shay's brain was swollen. It took three years of MRIs before detecting brain shrinkage. There was no way to get her on a plane in that condition. Shay's doctor was kind enough to contact the Mayo Clinic to send her lab results to them.

One of my friends had launched a GoFundMe campaign and raised $6,000 in less than forty-eight hours. During this time, many of my friends witnessed me, firsthand, deal with Shay's condition. I had been dragging her around with me everywhere, including to meetings, to keep a close eye on her.

After nearly a year of doctor's referrals and several weeklong hospitalizations, the Mayo Clinic finally had a treatment. They gave her three rounds of chemo. Chemo took her hair. Six months later, it ruined her teeth. As a result, the dentist pulled sixteen teeth. Today, her hair is still not growing in. She doesn't eat food. Her nutrition comes from a meal replacement, Ensure.

I thought my life was over as I knew it. I felt sorry for myself. My recent accomplishment of earning my bachelor's degree had me ready to take steps forward to search out a career. Despite a late start in life and being a non-traditional student, I was beginning to feel good about my life changes—you know, a girl like me with some years in recovery and getting her education. I looked forward to fulfilling the fantasy in my head about a new beginning. I was excited about it, and then *bam*, just like that, life changed in the blink of an eye. I moved out of my place and moved in with Shay and her kids out of consideration for their stability.

Without a second thought or any doubt, I set out to do what was in front of me to do. It took me a few years before I realized how immersed and narrowly focused I was on my daughter and grandchildren. I have spent my time observing what happened and recounting it to the doctors in real time. I came to terms with having no other personal goals besides being part of her healing. Because of her condition, Shay's ability to communicate was choppy. At times she could talk, and other times, she texted to communicate. Fortunately, she had learned sign language in high school and remembered it, so she could use it to communicate with others who knew it. The doctor says it's difficult to explain her brain damage. Being unable to take the brain apart makes it hard to pinpoint exactly which parts are affected by the damage. There were lots of things she could recall, but then there were times when she could not. The doctor shared with me an MRI that showed a distinctive mark that resembles the marking of an Alzheimer's patient.

Shay was assigned a team of doctors, a neurologist, a psychiatrist, a rheumatologist, an oncologist, and a primary care physician. Because my job has been to observe, learn about her basic care needs, take notes, and report, I've been treated like a team player by the medical professionals. We had visited the emergency department so many times that one time when we knew something was seriously wrong, her kids and I were so burnt out that we literally cried because none of us wanted to go again to sit for hours and hours. In that moment, I decided I was just not taking her to the emergency department anymore. I was just not going to do it. I was not going to deal with it. I kissed and hugged her, and then we all went to bed. I went to bed and pulled the covers over my head. Shay was super-loud the next morning. I again stubbornly refused to take her to the emergency room. Instead, I got her in the car and took her for a long ride. Taking her for a long ride often relieved us all from her whining and crying about her pain because it relaxed her. This time, we drove forty miles south to Alki Beach Park in Seattle. It was the first time I had ever been there, but I insisted on going to the beach. I thought the beach would be of great help for us all. I don't know why I thought that, but I did. I parked the car on the street in front of a pathway that led to the ocean. It was not a parking space, nor was it access to the water, so I looked for somebody I could ask about how to get to the beach park.

As I walked toward the water's edge, near the grassy area, I observed a woman walking toward me. I was excited to see someone since I had parked illegally and not many people were walking toward me. I said, "Excuse me, miss; can you tell me where the beach is?" The woman walked closer to me and took off her shades. It was the doctor who had told me to take Shay to the emergency room the night before. I couldn't believe it! I started telling her everything—I just started rapidly spilling the beans on myself about why I hadn't take Shay to the hospital like she suggested.

The doctor took her time, calmed me down, and told me where the beach was, but not before she sat down and gave me a professional doctor's session right there. We talked about how Shay was doing in the moment. She suggested we make an appointment with her for the next day and she would confirm it once she went into her office. What are the odds of running away from something I don't want to do, only to run into the doctor who told me what to do? I was being defiant. I had rushed all that way from home only to have the doctor who told me what to do be the one to walk up the path and greet me. That's my luck—period.

The next time we were at the psychiatrist's, I was talking like I always do when Shay started fiddling with her piece of paper much louder the usual. I stopped and asked, "Shay, do you want to talk?" She hardly ever used her words, but this time she used them well. She spoke clearly, saying, "My kids are mean to me. They always want me to be quiet because I do a lot of loud humming. I think they'll be better off without me. I hate my condition. I just want to gouge my eyes out. I'm so frustrated. I want to work, but there is no work I can do." And then she turned to me and said, "Mom, I'm sorry. I'm really sorry, Mom, that I feel this way."

Impressed by her words, the doctor asked, "Do you have a plan to hurt yourself?" She answered, "I think about hurting myself a lot. The only reason I don't is because of my family." The doctor asked, "Well, if you feel like hurting yourself, will you tell your mom?" She said, "Yeah, I'll tell my mom." Shay turned and looked at me and said, "Mom, I love you."

The session was over, but I was still bawling. Shay's pain touched me at the deepest part of my core. I've been living with her and witnessing her go through so many difficult challenges. She's lost nearly twenty-five pounds. She appears anorexic. She rarely eats solid foods anymore. She only drinks Ensure. She says it's the texture of food that prevents her from eating. Swallowing is an issue for her. Taking any kind of medication in pill form is out of the question. Because of the brain damage, she paces the floor day in and day out until she is worn out. Her voice is raised high and super-loud when she speaks. Brain damage has created the pseudobulbar affect, which makes her sound as if she is crying when she talks. Because of her brain trauma, she is forbidden to drive. Her MRI shows nerve damage. Her pain is consistent and continual. If you touch her in the slightest way, she screams that it hurts. We don't know if her brain exaggerates pain or if the pain actually happens. To have such a rude awakening at age twenty-seven, requiring such an overwhelming life change, is painful enough. Shay's cognitive piece was saved from brain damage, but it causes her more suffering. She is fully aware of all the changes because of her inability to control her behavior, her physical limitations, and her memory lapses. Understandably, she cries a lot.

That day when we left the doctor's office, I was trying to keep the tears from rolling down my face. By the time we reached the car, Shay said, "Mom, I'm so happy." I repeated her words, "You're happy?" She said, "Yeah, I feel better." Then she asked, "Are you okay?" How was I supposed to respond to that? "No, I'm not okay," I said. "I'm not okay at all. I'm really sad." I thought how I had worked so hard to make sure this girl had the best life she could have, but that wasn't enough. In that moment, I realized I could only do so much. It was significant for me to hear her express how she felt to her psychiatrist. Even though it broke my heart and I felt helpless, it dawned on me that it didn't matter what

I did, how much money I spent, how much time it took, or how much energy I had to exude—none of it mattered. The results remained up to God. I was overcome with overwhelming humility. I, for sure, am not God!

At the first sign of brain shrinkage from the MRI in 2018, Shay happened upon a very compassionate caregiver. This caregiver came in to work one day and, out of the blue, gifted Shay $500 and told her to make a wish. This caretaker was familiar with the Make-A-Wish Foundation, which I had never heard of before. It creates life-changing wishes for children with critical illnesses. Her grandson had passed away months before she took Shay on to care for. Shay randomly wished to go to Disneyland. I agreed to follow through with the wish. I got us plane tickets. With some skepticism, her kids and I got her on the plane. I knew right at takeoff that she would do fine. "Mom, this is beautiful," she said. She used the words. She felt a little independent from me once we got to Disneyland. It was like she was a kid with a new start all over again,

I decided to encourage her independence and help her get back to motherhood through more of these kinds of activities, such as taking her on short plane rides, driving her to the beach and hanging out, and asking her to watch over her kids. I've been watching little pivots where I see a change or two in her. I know I don't have the power to make her well, but keeping her brain as stimulated as possible has become satisfying enough. Here's an example of how magical this experience has been from a Facebook post I made on January 28, 2017:

Stepped Back

> I had a powerful lesson in taking a step back. Stepping back for me does not mean silently stewing

or passively agreeing on issues we face these days. Stepping back for me came in the form of recognizing and acknowledging.

Many of you know I have been dealing with my daughter and her children. Last night, a five-hour hospital visit revealed nuance. My daughter tells me she has a high level of anxiety. I see the change in her behavior when we are in crowds of people. My daughter tells me her sense of smell is gone; she cannot smell anything, I test the theory often to measure change. My daughter tells me her vision is blurred at times when she asks for help to read something. She tells me her hearing is messing up on her so that she cannot hear herself talking loudly. Evidence is there by the volume at which she listens to television and music. On many counts, I usually step up and advocate for her. But I discovered a measuring meter in my daughter last night when her daughter was sick that had me take a step back.

Shay fears everything, but her courage returns when her kids are involved. At the registration counter, I started answering questions as I have usually done over the past nineteen months. Shay piped up and started answering the questions. I immediately stepped back and silenced myself. I recognized and acknowledged her natural maternal instincts. When the doctor came in to examine Akiera Shay piped up again and requested some services for her daughter's protection and comfort that I never would have considered.

Case in point, never underestimate the power of a mother's love. I stepped back. She stepped up.

Taking care of Shay helped me experience the significance of love and tolerance at a deeper level. Shay puts into perspective many things that people take for granted. Witnessing her uphill struggle to do what comes naturally to adults who were not born with disabilities, like dressing herself, feeding herself, and taking herself to the rest room, have taken their toll on me. I developed the habit of waking up in the middle of night to make sure she was okay. Some days, it was really hard for me to know I had lost my daughter as I had once known her.

Many sleepless nights later, Shay started making noise when she woke to let me know she was awake. I went out of my way to make sure that I could get her anything at all she would be willing to eat. Hugs always made her feel better. Dozens of hugs a day became habitual. I did everything within my power. We didn't have a lot of money, but we went a lot of places and did a lot of things. I think that God allowed us to do that for Shay so she could make the best of the life she's got.

I managed day after day for more than three years before we got help from an outside caregiver. Once a caregiver was in place, my job became managing her caregivers. Keeping an eye out to ensure people are treating her kindly is a bit more work.

The doctor said her MRI shows a spot over her brain that's similar to that of an Alzheimer's patient. Shay forgets things sometimes. For example, we had just come back from the Grand Canyon when she asked where we had gone because she couldn't remember. She cries and cries when she can't remember things. And when she does remember something, she tells me that remembering makes her happy.

Even though I might not have the power to stop Shay from feeling her life is meaningless like she expressed, I can help her help herself. It's been both heartbreaking—and encouraging. Any small improvement makes me think, *Oh, my God, this is another sign that maybe she's getting well.* We see the slow progress her brain is making toward healing. No matter how small the increments, we celebrate them. She'll just out of the blue text me and say, "Mom, thank you so much." She says thank you for everything. She says she couldn't do this without me. When I get notes like that from her, they make everything we have gone through worth it. And it's been a lot—besides caring for her, at one point, I was working three part-time jobs. Besides running my own cleaning service, I worked at a hotel and a nonprofit recovery agency.

Over the years, the goal has remained the same: keeping Shay with her kids. She's slowly healing and watching them grow. Every so often, she texts me to say, "Mama, thank you so much. I don't know what I would do without you." And believe me, I get tons of texts like that from her. It cracks my heart wide open, and it makes me feel that sacrificing for the ones you love is not only worth it, but is my true purpose in living.

Six years after being in the psych ward, Shay told her psychiatrist how she felt about her condition. What she said was heartbreaking. "Although I deeply appreciate my mom, I feel bad that her time is taken up caring for me. I love my kids very much, but I feel bad for them. I'm not the same mom. I want to work and take care of myself and my kids. I remember I used to have a life. And when I think about it, I had some friends. We were really tight friends. I don't even get to see them anymore. They don't even call me because of my condition. My friends used to visit with me, not anymore. I feel like I am stuck in this condition, hopeless. There are times when I wish I weren't alive. I feel like I have no purpose in life." Listening to her speak about how she felt swelled my heart and made tears roll down my face uncontrollably.

During the coronavirus pandemic, it's been especially hard for Shay. Her whole life already had been narrowed down from her having her own apartment, working five days a week, visiting with her friends regularly, hanging out at the mall, and doing all this stuff on her own to being unable to do any of those things and not knowing when she ever will. She used to own two cars. I didn't even know she had a second car since she had worked and bought these things for herself. Now, she can't even drive because she is likely to have an accident, and it's going to be her fault because of her brain damage, right? Shay depends on other people to take her places. Many days, she has just wanted to go to the store, but I was too tired to take her. I couldn't even do it, you know—to push myself to do one more thing. Finally, she got a caregiver. I didn't even know how to deal with a caregiver, what to expect, or what to ask them to help with. I kept trying to do everything before they got there.

Shay has a caregiver right now, an eighty-three-year-old woman born and raised in Japan. I've thought, *She's eighty-three; we should be taking care of her*. Oh, no, this woman gets my daughter to do whatever she needs to do. She has skill at knowing how to handle Shay because with my daughter's brain damage, if you ask her to do one thing, she does just the opposite. If you want to see someone whose brain is out to get them, it's my daughter. It's very hard to watch it. If something is healthy for her to do, she'll do just the opposite. One time, the caregiver forgot to make sure Shay drank her Ensure, so she drank six or seven, maybe eight cups of coffee instead. She came home and fainted.

I love Shay. My grandkids are growing up. They are both in middle school. Let me see…my grandson will be fourteen in December; he was eight when Shay had her accident. Shay's daughter is eleven now, so she was five then. And boy, the accident was a change for them because they lost their mom as they knew her. Those kids are amazing because they have a way of explaining her condition to people that I couldn't match. I go through all these long explanations, but my granddaughter says, "My mom, her brain just got a little bit wiggly like this, and when her brain goes wiggly like that, then she can't do this business."

Wow. That's the way I have to describe her now. Her brain, you know, it kind of goes a little weird; when it goes weird, she does these things. It's okay. People have actually looked at Shay and stepped away, so Shay has gotten into the habit of saying beautiful things to people.

One time, we were on the road and stopped at a rest stop. We had to use the restroom, and I was telling Shay, "Please, just leave people alone. They don't understand. I don't want people to hurt you." Well, I don't know what she said to the woman at the rest stop, but I told Shay to come over back to the car and leave her alone. That woman ran to my car and said, "I just want you to know that what your daughter just said to me made my day." That helped me stop saying, "Shay, come over here," constantly trying to protect her from people.

I never knew how people would respond to her. Some reacted by stepping away from her. Others responded in kindness. Because of Shay's condition and because she consistently works hard to make connections with people, she's well known in the community. Everyone from store workers to EMTs (whom we have called many times) know who she is.

Once, when the town was having a parade, Shay wanted to go and begged me to let her stay to watch the parade alone. I didn't trust she could do it, but I was too tired to watch with her. I had worked three jobs that day. I explained to her that I wanted her to go, but I was too tired and could not take her. I had driven us to the store, believing she would follow me in as usual. Instead, she decided to walk off. I looked around and didn't see her anywhere. I called her phone, leaving three messages, but she didn't answer. I searched for her to no avail. I gave up, went home, called the cops, and continued calling her phone.

Finally, I stopped, prayed, and turned the situation over to a Higher Power. Eventually, Shay called to ask if she could stay at the parade. She had found a neighbor who agreed to bring her home after. I ceased fighting the idea since I was home. I spoke with the neighbor, who reassured me and kept me from worrying. I rationalized it was good for Shay to have a new experience after so many years of healing. I had to find out what she could do for herself. But I still called her phone every half hour to check on her. She didn't answer. Finally, my phone rang. Shay's name popped on the screen. I answered immediately. She said, "Mom, can you pick me up?"

I got in the car and rushed down to pick her up. I asked her what she had been doing. Shay had texted me saying she was *in* the parade. It turns out she was. The cops knew her from seeing her at the Y and around the community. She is pretty loud, so people notice her in public. The cops asked her if she wanted to be in the parade. They sat her in the backseat of the police car with the windows down as she held her hand outside the window, waving like she was Miss America. The whole time I was worried about her, she was recreating her life and having fun.

I have captured so many moments on camera for future reference. Someday we will look through the pictures and remember the good times we had in spite of the hard days where six hours in the emergency room was just another day in our new normal.

The lessons I've learned taking care of Shay, who in many ways reverted to being a small child who needed lots of attention and care, reassure me that love never fails, and love is never ending. When all else fails, compassion, kindness, and patience wins—every time, not sometimes. During the many moments when I was completely out of energy and felt as if I had nothing left to give, not even another breath to breathe, somehow, I inhaled one more breath of love and exhaled that which was given to me by so many people—the number is too large to count.

When I close my eyes now, no longer are the faces in Michael Jackson song "Black or White" unknown and unfamiliar. Those faces became real people's faces—I know their names, and many are written across my heart forever. Some died my heroes, and all left me holding the tiki torch to carry on my journey of recovery, awaiting my turn to pass it on.

I want to end with this poem I've written about the path of recovery.

Learn to live in solitude; meditate.

Cry when you have to; smile even when you don't want to.

Live outside the clique; keep your circle small.

Live uncomfortably to meet challenges.

Quit saying what you can't do; always speak about what you can do.

Keep learning; keep loving.

The Universe returns what you put out; speak positivity into the Universe.

Be the one who makes the difference and be a cheerleader.

Fear is debilitating; don't be afraid to make mistakes.

Listen intently; vent when you need to.

Live your values; stand ready to be influenced positively.

Be in the course of life; don't be a benchwarmer.

Write out your prayers; write out your goals.

Identify what motivates you.

Take risks.

You are who you say you are; now live it.

Say yes unless no is warranted.

Be spontaneous; remain flexible.

Think critically but fearlessly.

Co-create with God.

Lessons Learned

1. If you feel like you are struggling, keep pushing on.

2. If you feel like you can't breathe, stop and breathe.

Questions for Reflection

moment ward
called remember
used saying keep finally says
taken power okay use years started thought experience
caregiver lot condition know something god call
talk made brain makes shay's everything tells
accident emergency mom car
change love mri pain alone
stepped one times day time toward just wanted
shay kids back daughter go recovery feel job
lesions friends felt six asked good things woman
sure beach damage hospital looked doctor knew think
parade days life want next sign help work
taking went three even took high told people two
care left home first live hard
decided plane children around
months

Have you or a loved one experienced a life-changing event? How did you show up for that?

Have you ever been a caretaker to someone? What was rewarding about that experience?

What did you learn about life from someone who needed to be cared for?

A Final Note

I WANT YOU TO THINK DEEPLY AND critically about the last five to ten years of your life. When life is just shitty—meaning it seems pointless, unfair, or horrible—what do you do about it? Perhaps you've had people misunderstand you. Perhaps they haven't taken any time to get to know you, but have just made negative blanket statements about you. Perhaps they've even verbally abused, belittled, and humiliated you.

Perhaps, as a result, you have felt like your life is complete shit. Perhaps you feel like you don't even want to live anymore, but for some reason, you keep living. What do you do when you feel that way?

You could drink and drug to cope with your problems, to relieve stress and momentarily escape. You could self-medicate to reduce feelings of anger and hurt, loneliness and boredom, to cover up your lack of confidence with a feeling of being alive. But I can tell you from experience that those so-called solutions only create more problems. The answer is starting to acknowledge how you feel.

Most people don't want to talk about their emotions. Most prefer to stuff their feelings. As a result, most people stay stuck, unable to change.

Change requires trusting someone. Trusting is not easy, not when we've learned not to trust. Not when we've trusted in the past, only to find it resulted in more harm than help.

Still, trusting someone is the beginning of the answer. Do you have one friend or family member who will support you? Do you want to change your life? Do you believe you can do this alone? Has trying to do it on your own been working for you so far?

You can't do it on your own, and guess what? You are not alone. I want you to know that I know your pain. I have been in your shoes. I know what it's like to go through a crisis alone. I know what's it's like not to have anyone you can trust to talk to. I felt like no one understood me. I felt like no one was there to hear me. I have walked miles in your shoes. Eventually, I had to face the fact that I could not guide myself alone.

In my story, you have learned how the Universe guided me once I decided to let it. Friends appeared and doors opened once I was ready to accept help.

The same can happen for you. But you must be willing to do some things you do not want to do. For example, take some directions from people who can help you—a friend, a doctor, a counselor, an AA group, a pastor—whoever you feel you can trust. Follow through on those directions even if you feel uncomfortable and or awkward. Recovery is a process of fact finding and fact facing. It takes courage to face facts. Your addiction will tell you that you cannot dare to look for help, but with courage, you will break down the barriers to your personal goals and your recovery.

You and I have lived through trauma most of our lives. Turning our attention toward healing takes more than the desire; it requires action. The first three principles to a successful recovery are honesty, open-mindedness, and willingness. First things first. Admitting to yourself and another human being that you need help is the first step. Trust will follow in small increments until you fully understand you can trust the creator of this universe. Every step in recovery is a new learning experience, sometimes exciting, sometimes reflective; either way, every step and every day is worth it. You, too, can discover your values, your voice, and your own worth.

You are worthy!

About the Author

WINONNA SAARI WAS BORN AND RAISED in Black Bottom, a community in Detroit, Michigan. She has a BA in Communication and is working on an MA in Clinical Mental Health Counseling.

As a single mother—and now grandmother—Winonna has overcome trauma, tragedy, and addiction. Growing up in the inner city, Winonna learned first-hand the impact of living with untreated mental illness, little support, and an overall unhealthy environment. Winonna's sheer determination and many leaps of faith turned her life around. Today, as a freelance journalist and certified recovery coach, she assists a community challenged with rampant addiction and untreated mental health issues.

Winonna has experienced the effects of growing up with fear from childhood trauma and growing up in the inner city. Unknowingly, she lived with early onset alcoholism and drug addiction. Although she's lived through heartbreaking tragedy, amid her despair was born desperation, which led to her path of recovery. Her past met her present. Her high school friends met her newfound friends. Her friendships remain pillars. Her courage and risk-taking determination, along with her leaps and bounds of faith and adventures eventually led her to hope, inspiration, purpose, and being a woman of worth.

Hire Winonna to Speak at Your Next Event

WHEN IT COMES TO CHOOSING A professional speaker for your next event, you will find no one more respected or successful—no one who will leave your audience or colleagues inspired, hopeful, completely filled with passion, and ready to create the life of their dreams than Winonna Saari. Winonna offers the guidance and accountability of an experienced recovery coach, and she has been presenting to audiences all over Western Washington's I-5 corridor.

Winonna knows you want a memorable speaker who will leave your audience eager to take initiative toward life changes. As a result, Winonna's speaking philosophy is to humor, entertain, and inspire your audience with passion and stories proven to help people achieve extraordinary results.

Whether your audience is 10 or 10,000, Winonna Saari will deliver a customized message of inspiration and hope for your meeting or conference. She will humor, entertain, and inspire your audience with her warm and passionate style.

If you are looking for an unforgettable speaker, consider booking Winonna Saari.

www.WomanofWorthBook.com

Made in the USA
Coppell, TX
18 November 2021